Acknowledgments

Writing this book has been a labor of love, and I could not have accomplished it without the help and encouragement of others. I would like to acknowledge the following:

Roland Levesque, my husband. You patiently endured my long hours in front of the computer and the frequent times of eating out. Thank you.

Frances Keiser, Sagaponack Books & Design. Without your expertise, I would have been lost trying to get this book published. You have been a lifesaver! Thank you.

Beth Mansbridge, copyeditor. Thank you for the hours of correcting grammatical errors to make this book presentable. I appreciate your diligence and the encouraging words.

Jack Schneider, a former pastor. I treasure that you instilled in me a love of God's Word and encouraged me to write.

Dr. David Beauchamp, current pastor. Thank you for faithfully preaching God's Word and for your love, prayers, support, and encouragement.

I also offer my heartfelt gratitude to Jeannine Auth, Jeanne Dennis, Linda Farley, Carla McCargo, and Kathy Sanchez, who have faithfully prayed for me and encouraged me while I wrote this book.

I thank you, the reader, for choosing to read *Praying Through the Psalms*. I pray that you will be blessed as you spend time in prayer.

Ultimately, all praise and thanks go to God the Father, Son, and Holy Spirit.

Jesus said, "I am the vine, you are the branches; he who abides in Me and I in him, he bears much fruit, for apart from Me you can do nothing."

I dedicate this book first and foremost to God. Without Him, nothing exists and life is meaningless.

To my family, whom I dearly love: Roland, my husband; Renee, daughter; Michelle and Adam, daughter and son-in-law; and Alyssa and Adam, our grandchildren.

To my spiritual family, my brothers and sisters in Christ.

To all the precious people God has brought into my life over the years, who have influenced my life in some way. I pray God will richly bless you.

Preface

All scripture is inspired by God and profitable for teaching, for reproof, for correction, for training in righteousness; so that the man of God may be adequate, equipped for every good work. 2 Timothy 3:16–17

For the word of God is living and active and sharper than any two-edged sword, and piercing as far as the division of the soul and spirit, of both joints and marrow, and able to judge the thoughts and intentions of the heart. Hebrews 4:12

These two verses are the foundation for this book. All Scripture quotations are from the New American Standard Bible.

God Almighty, Creator of this universe, created man in His image and inspired His written love letter to reveal Himself to us. The Bible not only details His power, sovereignty, holiness, and righteousness, but also His infinite love and care for all mankind. His written Word provides direction as to how we are to live and have fellowship with Him and others. Obedience to His Word is the key to a fulfilling life that brings honor and glory to God. The Word of God is living and powerful, and God the Holy Spirit convicts us of sin, judgment, and righteousness.

God the Father longs to have fellowship with us and He sent His Son Jesus to restore the fellowship that was broken by our sin. His death on the cross was the acceptable sacrifice so that our sins can be forgiven and our fellowship restored with Almighty God. As with any relationship, both parties involved must communicate with one another. A good relationship is never one-sided. As I read God's Word, the Lord speaks to me and I must respond. My first response is prayer. I talk to the Lord about what I am reading and what He is saying to me personally. And then, after prayer, He reveals to me the application.

I have written *Praying Through the Psalms* because I firmly believe that prayer and Bible reading go hand in hand. The following are my recorded prayers in response to God as He has spoken to my heart through the Psalms. This book is intended to be a companion as you read the Psalms from your own Bible. As you read the Bible, listen to what God is saying to you personally and then respond to Him. I have chosen the Psalms because the focus is praising God; however, the concept of prayer applies to all Scripture. As you read the Psalms, these prayers may express your heart and you can pray them to your Heavenly Father, Who hears. God may say something completely different to you, so change, add, and subtract words as you fellowship with your Heavenly Father. My prayers are simple. They are not eloquent or wordy, but God is not as concerned with our words as He is our hearts. The goal is fellowship with a loving Father—a personal relationship with Almighty God, through faith in Jesus Christ.

It is my sincere prayer that you will be blessed as you pray through the Psalms with me.

Open my eyes that I may behold wonderful things from Your Law. Psalm 119:18

Included in this book are Hebrew names of God which reveal different facets of His character. They more fully describe God's qualities and Who He really is. Also included is a collection of sunrises that I have personally taken with either my phone or camera. Each one is a photo taken from behind my home. As you will see, each sunrise is unique and designed by our artistic Creator and Heavenly Father. Each sunrise reveals an awesome God!

PRAYING THROUGH THE PSALMS

He will be like a tree firmly planted by streams of water, which yields its fruit in its season and its leaf does not wither; and in whatever he does, he prospers. Psalm 1:3

Prayer Response to Psalm 1

Oh God, my Savior and Lord, I have learned that true joy and blessings come when I delight in You and Your Word. Your Word contains the answers to all my needs. There is never a reason to seek counsel from those who do not know You and are not obeying Your Word, because You have provided the Holy Spirit to be my counselor. Help me stay on Your righteous path and keep me from being discouraged with those who deny You and scoff at Your Word. Your love letter is precious to me and I love to meditate on it during the day and sometimes in the late hours of the night.

It is truly my desire to be like that tree firmly planted near the water, whose roots are deep and strong. Enable me to be deeply rooted in You and to be like that fruitful tree which bears the fruit of the Spirit and remains healthy and strong in You. Your Word reminds me that I am the branch and Jesus is the vine. I must remain attached to Him all the time because apart from Jesus I can do nothing. He is my lifeline. Keep me close to You, Lord.

Those who reject You are like chaff easily tossed about with the wind. They have no roots and no foundation. Sadly, when judgment comes, they will not be able to endure. They will not be able to withstand the storms of life without Your strength, mercy, and grace.

I pray for my loved ones who have rejected Jesus. He is the Way, the Truth, and the Life. No one can come to You except through Him. Have mercy on them, Father, and reveal to them their need for salvation. I am eternally grateful that I belong to You and can have fellowship with You. What a comfort and joy to my heart!

Fearfully, those who continue in their sinful ways and reject Jesus will perish because they have no hope. Draw them unto salvation by Your Holy Spirit. It is not Your will that any should perish. Thank You, Lord, for saving me.

El Yeshuati ... The God of My Salvation

Worship the Lord with reverence and rejoice with trembling.
Psalm 2:11

Prayer Response to Psalm 2

Sovereign Lord, it is You Who raises up our leaders and it is You Who deposes them. Yet, so many of our leaders fail to understand their inadequacies and fail to acknowledge You as Lord. Power, greed, and pride fill their hearts and they do not seek You or Your instruction. Many of our leaders deliberately reject Your ways and persecute those who desire to follow You. They make decisions based on personal power and advancement of their cause instead of the welfare of the people. But even so, You are still on the throne.

Jesus, You are the King of Kings and Lord of Lords, and will one day return to earth to claim what is rightfully Yours. You will establish real peace and will have the last word. All things were created by You and for You.

Jesus, You came initially as our suffering Savior to bear the sins of a lost world and to make a way for us to be right with God the Father. But when You come again You will come as our righteous Judge. You, oh Lord, will make things right. As Your judgments come upon this earth, open the eyes of our leaders and reveal to them their mortality and their need for Your wisdom, discernment, and guidance. You alone are worthy of our reverence, worship, and obedience.

Father, help each of us, and especially our leaders, to honor and obey You so that we can avoid Your discipline and judgment. Oh God, thank You for being our refuge and strength. Help our leaders to believe and trust in You so that we might lead a quiet and peaceful life. You, Lord Jesus, are the Prince of Peace. Thank You for the peace I have in You.

Shalom ... God Is Peace

But You, O Lord, are a shield about me, my glory, and the One who lifts my head. Psalm 3:3

Prayer Response to Psalm 3

D ear Father in heaven, I know that David was running from actual people who wanted to harm him. Thankfully, I am not aware that I have such enemies. But I do face the enemy of my soul each day. He uses people, health, things, and circumstances to try and cause me to doubt Your great love and to turn me away from You. From time to time, I forget about my spiritual enemy and fail to recognize his schemes. I sometimes fail to utilize all of the spiritual weapons You have given me: Your helmet of salvation, the breastplate of righteousness, the shield of faith, the sword of the spirit (which is Your Word), Your truth, and the gospel of peace. I find myself questioning when deliverance will come.

But Father, I have learned that You alone are my shield, my Rock, and my hiding place. You hear me when I cry out to You and You lift me up when I am down. Lord, You impart Your peace and give me rest in the night. You are the One Who sustains me. There is never a need to be afraid because You alone are God Almighty and my Heavenly Father. You have promised to never leave nor forsake me, and You have already won the victory. Thank You for Your great salvation. Thank You for Jesus. There is salvation in no other. I belong to You and my life is in Your hands. You have blessed me with every spiritual blessing in the heavenly places. I praise You that You are forever with me and provide my every need.

Jehovah Jireh ... The Lord Will Provide

But know that the Lord has set apart the godly man for Himself; the Lord hears when I call to Him. Psalm 4:3

Prayer Response to Psalm 4

My God and Savior, You are righteous in all Your ways. I am humbled and blessed that You, a righteous and holy God, hear and answer my prayers. I come to You in the name of Jesus. You are gracious and kind to me, and I am thankful that You grant me peace in the midst of my storms. Help me to always focus on You and not my circumstances. Keep me from being overly concerned about what others say, think, or do. So many people leave You out of their lives, but I cannot imagine life without You.

Lord, You called me before the foundation of the earth and set me apart for Your divine purposes. Keep Your calling ever in my mind and help me, Father, to be faithful to You. May I continually honor You in word, thought, and action, and please keep me from sin.

Lord, I love Your Word and I meditate on it and You throughout the day. As I do this, teach me to be still and listen to You. Help me to cease striving and wait upon You. Lord, You are not interested in material sacrifices or promises, but You are interested in my heart. Keep my heart in tune with Yours. Continue to mold me to be what You have called me to be.

You are the potter, and I am the clay. I recognize that my righteousness is as filthy rags, and my only righteousness is in Christ. Grant me grace to trust You in all things and let my life be a witness of Your saving grace. Father, You have placed within me a joyful heart, and I praise You. You give me Your peace so that when I lie down at night I sleep. I know You will keep me safe in Your arms. Thank You for being my Heavenly Father. I love You, Lord.

El Chaiyai ... The God of My Life

For it is You who blesses the righteous man, O Lord, You surround him with favor as with a shield. Psalm 5:12

Prayer Response to Psalm 5

Dear God, so many times I cry out to You with my doubts, fears, and complaints. You always patiently listen to the deep groaning of my heart. Thank You for Your ever-abiding presence and Your attention to me. As I awake each morning and lift my voice to You, I ask You to lead and guide my day. I wait and watch to see what You are doing in and through me and in the lives of others. I pray that You will keep me from wrong actions, wrong thinking, and speech that displeases and dishonors You.

Father, You are so holy, and I am so prone to sin and fall short of Your glory every day. Lord, I seek Your grace and deliverance from those sins that easily trip me up. Cleanse my heart from all pride. I have nothing to be boastful about. All that I am and have are gifts from You. Make me a person of integrity, always speaking the truth in love. Because of Your holiness, You hate all sin and do not distinguish between big and small sins. Help me to maintain Your Word in my heart so that I will not sin against You. Enable me to keep close accounts with You.

Thank You for Your promise that I will not be tempted beyond what I am able to overcome and that You will provide the way of escape. I praise You for Your abundant love, kindness, grace, and mercy. When I enter Your house of worship, may I honor, reverence, and worship You. Lord, guide and direct me into righteousness. Keep me on the straight and narrow path. There are so many people all around me who are selfish and self-centered, full of lies and deceit and rebellious against You. Lord, nothing escapes Your notice and You will hold everyone accountable one day because You are righteous and just.

Thank You for being my refuge. Your arms are always open wide and ready to shelter me through the storms of life. Father, I praise You and thank You for all Your blessings. Thank You for loving me and surrounding me with Your favor. I praise You, Lord!

El Channun ... The Gracious God

The Lord has heard my supplication, the Lord receives my prayer. Psalm 6:9

Prayer Response to Psalm 6

Heavenly Father, there have been times in my life when I have sensed that You are angry with me. Sometimes, Lord, that feeling has been justified. Many times, I am just perplexed because of the circumstances of life. Life really is not fair, and I do not understand why certain things happen—why people say and do the things they do. I question why people are sometimes so hateful and hurtful.

There are times that I wonder if You are chastising me or pruning me. Either way, Lord, it is uncomfortable and I cry out to You, "How long will this continue?" Then I think about what You are trying to show me, what You are working in my life. You remind me not to question but to trust You. Because I so desire to be close to You, I appeal to Your grace, mercy, and loving-kindness.

Lord, when I focus on my circumstances, I become weary and my strength is depleted. I become overly emotional and I am grieved. Thank You for reminding me that I belong to You and I need to return my focus on Jesus, the author and finisher of my faith. You have never left me nor forsaken me. You have heard my cries, seen my distress, and are acutely aware of all my circumstances. You remind me that You are still sovereign and in control of all things. Nothing has escaped Your notice and nothing happens without Your allowance. You, oh Lord, will guide and direct my circumstances and will use them for Your honor and glory and for my good.

I praise You for Your faithfulness and I thank You for all Your promises in Your Word. Thank You, Holy Spirit, for bringing them to mind when I need them. I praise You for being my loving Heavenly Father Who never rejects me, even when I am at my worst. Thank You for Your great love and forgiveness. You are Lord of all!

Adonai ... Lord

I will give thanks to the Lord according to His righteousness and will sing praise to the name of the Lord Most High. Psalm 7:17

Prayer Response to Psalm 7

Lord and Most High God, who have I in heaven but You? You are my refuge and strength. I run to You with all my struggles, and You hide me under the shadow of Your wings. David had enemies pursuing him, trying to kill him. I have an unseen spiritual enemy who constantly seeks to draw me away from You. Your Word reveals that he seeks to devour me! He sometimes uses people to try and discourage me, undermine me, and get me off track. But Father, I must bring every injustice to You: every unkind word, falsehood, and misinterpretation. You alone know the intentions of every heart.

Help me not to harbor ill feelings toward those who do this, because that, too, is sin. Empower me not to react but to respond like Jesus. Enable me to trust You to deal with every real or imagined enemy according to Your Word. You alone are righteous and just, and You know my heart. Check it and reveal to me when my heart is out of sync.

Lord, Your Word plainly states that I have a deceitful heart and I do not even know what lurks in there. Cleanse my heart and then help me to leave in Your care those who say and do things to harm or discredit me. Lord, You alone are the righteous Judge and You will wisely judge all things. Lord, I cannot convict, convince, or change others. Only You can convince people of sin, righteousness, and judgment. I ask that my integrity remains intact and that my heart is clean before You.

Father, show me my sin so that I can confess it and repent. Lord, You judge all unconfessed sins, and Your Word tells me that my sins will find me out. Nothing escapes Your notice, and many times people fall into their own sinful trap. Protect me, Lord, from myself, and give me Your grace to trust You to deal with others. I praise You for Your righteousness and I praise You that You, alone, are Lord Most High.

El Elyon ... Most High God

O Lord, our Lord, how majestic is Your name in all the earth!
Psalm 8:9

Prayer Response to Psalm 8

Glorious Lord, Your majesty is seen throughout the heavens and on earth and in the sea. I see Your splendor every morning as I look to the east and see Your beautiful sunrise. Your glory is seen in all of creation and I do not have to look far to see Your handiwork. Even now, Lord, as I hear the birds singing and enjoy the gentle breezes of the wind, I am reminded that You not only created it all, but hold it all together! You are sovereign and in control of all things.

And Lord, You created more than the things that are seen. When I consider the vastness of the universe, I am completely in awe! When I look at my own body, I cannot help but know I am a miracle! I am fearfully and wonderfully made. And when I realize that there are billions of people on this earth and no one person is alike, how awesome is that! Your majesty, Lord, is beyond all comprehension! And then, to think that in all the vast universe You love and care about me, a speck of dust in comparison!

I am reminded that I am created in Your image and I was chosen in Christ, before the foundation of the earth, for a specific purpose. Grant me Your power to fulfill that purpose. I thank You for the promise that it is You Who began a good work in me and it is You Who will complete it.

All of creation was created by Jesus and for His pleasure. And one day Jesus is coming back and will take His rightful place as King of Kings and Lord of Lords. When that happens, every knee will bow and every tongue will confess that Jesus is Lord. How majestic is Your name, oh Lord! May my life bring honor and glory to You.

El Hakkavod ... The God of Glory

And those who know Your name will put their trust in You,
for You, O Lord, have not forsaken those who seek You.
Psalm 9:10

Prayer Response to Psalm 9

God Almighty, my heart overflows with thanksgiving. You continue to amaze me in numerous ways. I rejoice in You and sing songs of praise to You, my God, my Heavenly Father, Savior, Lord, and friend. You have sustained me and protected me my entire life. You sit on Your throne and reign as a righteous Judge. You witness all things good and bad and You judge accordingly.

Lord, I have personally experienced Your blessings and Your discipline. Your Word tells me that You discipline those Whom You love, and I know that You love me. You even rebuke the nations when they continue to reject You and Your Word. Sadly, those who continue to reject You, their names are blotted out of the Book of Life. What a tragic and unnecessary commentary. After death, we are all eventually forgotten, but You are not. You are everlasting and Your judgments are pure and equitable. Who can question You?

Thank You for being a stronghold for those who are discouraged and oppressed. I have been there, Lord, and You have lifted me up. You have strengthened me in times of trouble, and I have claimed Your promise, that You never leave those who belong to You. I praise You that You are forever with me.

Give to me Your power and embolden me to share with others Your wonderful deeds. Enable me to convey to others that You have not forgotten anyone and are always listening to those who call upon You. You are acutely aware of our afflictions and You care. Absolutely nothing ever escapes Your notice.

Thank You for Your abundant grace that we all so desperately need. In the midst of affliction, strengthen me to sing Your praises to others and enable me to rejoice in Your salvation. Thank You, Lord, for saving my soul.

You have revealed Yourself to all peoples through creation, so everyone is without excuse. Yet despite divine revelation, there are many who still trust in their own good works and are determined to ignore You and Your plan of salvation through faith in Jesus. Father, Your judgment comes sooner or later to those who continue to reject You. Draw them to Yourself.

Lord, You see the needy and the afflicted. They are everywhere. You are also mindful, Father, that we are mortal beings, created from dust. I appeal to Your mercy and acknowledge that You are righteous in Your dealings with us.

Oh Father, if only all of mankind would have a reverent fear of You. You are God Almighty and worthy of all praise! You are Alpha and Omega, the beginning and the end!

El Shaddai ... God Almighty

O Lord, You have heard the desire of the humble; You will strengthen their heart, You will incline Your ear. Psalm 10:17

Prayer Response to Psalm 10

Most holy and righteous God, there have been times in my life when You have seemed so far away. Yet Your Word reminds me that You are everywhere. Your presence surrounds me, no matter where I am and no matter what is going on. However, I do understand why so many people have questions.

This world is so sinful and chaotic and people all around the world are involved in all kinds of evil. So many people have lost all regard for the lives of others. People everywhere are selfish, prideful, greedy, and they deny You, and yet they still seem to prosper. These same people do not consider You at all. They live as though they are in control and invincible. They appear to be convinced that they can handle life on their own. They are deceitful, oppressive, full of mischief and wickedness, and take advantage of others who are less fortunate. They act as if You do not see or do not care, and some even say that You do not exist. When others see these injustices, they begin to doubt Your great love.

Oh Lord, I know that You see and know all things and are in control of all things. You are sovereign, omnipotent, omnipresent, and omniscient. I am convinced that You are loving, gracious, kind, holy, and righteous, and that You hear the cries of the oppressed. I know because I have been there. You hear the prayers of the humble and You strengthen them. I praise You for strengthening me when I have needed it.

You are a loving Father to the orphans. And yes, Lord, You see the wicked and will one day judge their deeds accordingly. But You are loving and patient and desiring these same people to repent and turn to You. Oh Lord, open people's eyes to the truth of Your Word. Enlighten their hearts and minds to the Gospel. The reason there is so much turmoil in our world is because people have rejected Jesus. They have rejected You and Your ways.

Your Word provides the answer to all of life's questions and shows us how we should live. We live in a sin-cursed world, but You have provided a way for everyone to be right with You and others. Your Word tells us that way is Jesus. Thank You for sending to us a loving Savior. Open the eyes of those who have rejected Jesus and use me to spread the Good News to those who have not heard. Help me to be faithful in sharing Jesus with others and may my life reflect Him.

Until Jesus returns and restores peace, I know there will continue to be injustice. But one day You will judge the earth in righteousness and all things will be made right. Even so, come, Lord Jesus!

El Tsaddik ... The Righteous God

For the Lord is righteous, He loves righteousness; the upright will behold His face. Psalm 11:7

Prayer Response to Psalm 11

You, Lord Jesus, are my refuge. When the enemy tries to destroy me, I fly like a bird to You! You alone are my solid foundation. You are the beginning and the end and everything in between. I am eternally secure in You.

Jesus, You are sitting at the right hand of the Father, seeing all things and testing the hearts of the wicked and the righteous. You even intercede on my behalf. How awesome that is!

Lord, You pour out Your love and blessing upon me, and I am so thankful. I look forward to the day when I will see You face-to-face. I pray for those who do not know You, especially in my family. In Your mercy, draw them unto salvation. You are a gracious and merciful God, slow to anger and rich in mercy! I praise You that I belong to You.

El Malei Rachamim ... All Merciful God

Prayer Response to Psalm 12

God of heaven and earth, like David, I ask for Your help. I seek Your divine intervention in the affairs of my family, our nation, and the world. I am sometimes overwhelmed with the turmoil and wickedness that goes on constantly all around me, and it seems that fewer and fewer people acknowledge You, let alone seek You.

Lord, even those who call themselves Christians do not always speak the truth. Family members lie consistently and do it without any conscience. As I listen to the news it is difficult to discern truth from falsehood. Neighbors and friends have become pathological liars and I cry out to You for discernment. Your Word says to speak the truth in love, and yet so many people speak from hearts that are uncaring, selfish, and unkind. They speak words that will benefit them, with no regard as to how their words affect others.

Oh God, You see and hear all things. Protect Your children from the lies that permeate our world. And Father, please help me to courageously speak truth. Convict and convince those who lie, of their sin, righteousness, and the judgment to come. Lord, I look to Your Word for wisdom, discernment, guidance, understanding, and strength. Your Word alone is absolute truth and will last forever. Those who lie may be praised and exalted in this life, but You, Lord, will have the final word. Have mercy on those who continue in their sin. Convict them, help them to repent, and draw them to Jesus. Jesus, You are the Way, the Truth, and the Life. I praise You that You are Truth.

El Emet ... The God of Truth

The fool has said in his heart, there is no God. Psalm 14:1

Prayer Response to Psalm 13

Sovereign Lord, there have been times in my life when I have felt like David. It seems as if You have hidden Yourself from me. My prayers seem to go unanswered and I think I will be overcome by the circumstances that bombard my life. However, as I read Your Word, You remind me that I belong to You. You remind me of Your great love. I am reminded that the righteous will not be shaken. My heart is strengthened by Your magnificent salvation in Christ, and I praise You.

Father, You are so gracious and merciful to me. And I am reminded that You cause all things to work together for my good—the good, the bad, and the ugly. I praise You for Your providential care.

Yaweh ... Sovereign Lord

Prayer Response to Psalm 14

Heavenly Father, I come before You, acknowledging that You are God Almighty, Creator of heaven and earth. There are so many people all around me that reject You. They think I am foolish, Lord, because I love You and want to follow You. But Your Word says they are the fools. Their hearts are cold and evil, and their actions reveal what is in their hearts.

You, in Your holiness, see that we are all sinners. None of us are righteous within ourselves. You make it plain that not a single person consistently does good. You are looking for those who recognize their wretchedness and will seek You. Lord, open the eyes of my family, friends, and neighbors so that they might understand. Enlighten their hearts to see themselves as sinners in need of a Savior. Reveal to them that judgment is coming and give them a desire to call out to You for salvation.

Father, thank You for revealing to me my sinfulness and my need for Jesus. Thank You for drawing me to Jesus and saving my soul. Jesus alone is my refuge and salvation.

When Jesus returns, all things will be restored and Your chosen nation of Israel will recognize Jesus as Messiah. Oh Father, open the eyes of Your chosen people, that they might see.

El Yisrael ... The God of Israel

O Lord, who may abide in Your tent? Who may dwell on Your holy hill? He who walks with integrity, and works righteousness. Psalm 15:1

Prayer Response to Psalm 15

Lord God, I desire to be a person of integrity. Enable me to always speak truth and do the things I know are right and pleasing to You. Lord, hold me close to You and keep my heart clean. Father, guard my heart, mouth, and actions so that I will not say or do anything that would harm my neighbor, family, or friends. If I should give in to the temptation to do so, please convict my heart immediately and give me the grace to confess and repent. Guide me on the straight and narrow path.

Father, I desire to honor You with my life. Help me not to hold grudges when I am hurt, and to readily forgive and move on. Change my heart in those areas that need to be changed. I realize I do not even know my own heart, so I am trusting You to examine me and reveal to me those things that are not right.

Father, strengthen me and help me to be more loving and generous. You have so richly blessed me in so many ways. Give me the desire to share those blessings with others. And when I do give, Lord, help me to do it privately and joyously, expecting absolutely nothing in return. Jesus gave His life for me. The least I can do is give back to You what is rightfully already Yours.

Lord, You are my solid foundation. If I remain close to You and obey Your Word, Your promise is that I will not be easily shaken. I praise You that no one and nothing can snatch me out of Your hand! I am secure in Jesus.

El Sali ... The God of My Strength

I said to the Lord, "You are my Lord; I have no good besides You." Psalm 16:2

Prayer Response to Psalm 16

You alone are God Almighty and my only refuge. Jesus, You are Lord of my life and You are my righteousness. I praise You that I have been adopted into Your kingdom and I am a child of the King!

Father, protect me from the idols of my heart that try to draw my attention away from You. Things and people never satisfy. They are temporal and often bring about heartache and sorrow. My inheritance is in You, Lord, and it is You Who fills my cup with joy. You alone sustain my life and bless my heart. I thank You for the life that You have given to me. I cannot thank You enough for Your Word as it counsels, instructs, and ministers to me in numerous ways.

Lord, keep my heart and mind focused on Jesus, the author and finisher of my faith. It is impossible to understand, but since Jesus is at Your right hand and I am in Jesus, I am there also! How awesome! I am completely secure in Christ. Just as Jesus conquered death and rose from the grave, I, too, will rise from the grave—that is, if I die before Christ returns.

I praise You for revealing to me Your great salvation and assuring me that I will spend eternity in heaven with Jesus. Father, I already experience such joy and peace in Your presence. I cannot imagine what it will be like when I see You face-to-face! What a day that will be!

El Olam ... The Everlasting God

Keep me as the apple of the eye; hide me in the shadow of Your wings. Psalm 17:8

Prayer Response to Psalm 17

Father, I praise You that You are a righteous and just God. I am so grateful that You hear my prayers and, more importantly, You know my heart. I ask, Lord, that You guard my mouth from sinful words and that my actions will reflect Jesus. Keep me firmly grounded in Your Word so that I will stay on the narrow road and not veer off track.

Not only do I praise You for hearing my prayers, but I thank You for answering them. You answer each one in Your time and according to Your perfect will and purposes. Forgive me when I am impatient and for the times that I doubt.

I praise You, Lord, for Your great love and kindness, and for my undeserved salvation. You are my refuge and my hiding place. God, I am so blessed and You have shown great favor to me over the years. You have protected me more often than I know.

Lord, there is so much hate and wickedness in this world, so I pray for those who are uncaring and proud, and I lift before You those who deliberately try to harm others. Jesus told us to love our enemies and pray for those who persecute us. Only the power of Your Holy Spirit can enable me to do that.

I also pray for those who desire only the things of this world. Draw them to Jesus and reveal to them that this world is passing away. Enable them to see that only in Christ is found abundant and eternal life. I cannot change others or the world. Only Jesus can do that. But I do need to be faithful in sharing Christ with others. Forgive me for the many times I fail.

Enable me to keep my eyes on Jesus and keep me from sin. Help me to be content as I strive to be more like Jesus each day. Oh Father, You have promised to complete the work which You started in me. I praise You that I can rest in Jesus.

El Tsaddik ... Righteous God

For who is God, but the Lord? And who is a rock, except our God? Psalm 18:31

Prayer Response to Psalm 18

I come before You, acknowledging You as my Lord and Savior and Heavenly Father. You already know my heart, but I just want to tell You that I love You, Lord. You are my strength, my Rock, my fortress, and deliverer. You alone are my refuge and shield, the horn of my salvation and stronghold. I praise You because You alone are worthy of all praise.

It is You Who hears and answers my prayers. In times of need You have protected, strengthened, encouraged, and delivered me. When I call out to You for help You are always there, and You remain ever so close. Lord, You are all-powerful and able to do far more than I could possibly think or ask. The fact that You delight in me is beyond my understanding and I am humbled and yet so thankful.

Father, I am acutely aware that the only righteousness I have is in Jesus. When You look at me You see Him. Thank You, Jesus, that I can come to the Father completely blameless, in Your name. And thank You for the sweet fellowship we enjoy.

Father, You light my way and guide and direct my steps. Your Word is a lamp unto my feet and a light unto my path. You empower me with Your strength and keep me on the right path. You have saved me and Your right hand upholds me. I belong to You. No matter what enemies I face, Lord, I am never alone. You never leave nor forsake me. I entrust myself to You, the living and only Almighty God! I bless Your name and praise You that You are my all in all. You are a loving and kind Father. How wonderful You are!

El Hannora ... Awesome God

Let the words of my mouth and the meditation of my heart be acceptable in Your sight, O Lord, my rock and my Redeemer. Psalm 19:14

Prayer Response to Psalm 19

Awesome God, as I look out my window, everything I see and hear reminds me how awesome You are. The heavens are vast and endless. The clouds continuously change and form unique and beautiful designs. The sun miraculously arises each morning at Your appointed time and travels from east to west each day. Every night the moon and the stars light up the sky, just as You ordained. All of creation declares Your glory. How can anyone doubt that You are God!

Father, this Psalm reminds me of why I love Your Word so much. It reminds me that Your Word is perfect, sure, right, pure, everlasting, true, righteous, desirable, and sweet. John reminds me that Your words are spirit and they are life! Lord, spending time with You in Your perfect law truly restores my soul. It reminds me of Your greatness and goodness and that You have created me for a purpose. It gives me a deep sense of peace within.

Your Word refreshes me and prepares me to face the challenges of the day. I can depend upon Your testimonies to give me wisdom and insight as I face decisions and make judgments. Your precepts encourage my heart and give me inner joy. Your commandments supply me with spiritual understanding and guidance. And yes, Lord, sometimes Your Word warns me and convicts me of sin.

Your Word teaches me Who You are and causes me to humble myself before You. Everything in Your Word is true and right, and I absolutely love it because You speak to me personally and I draw ever so close to You.

Father, please guard my heart and my mouth. Out of my heart flow the issues of life and what comes out of my mouth reveals my heart. Let my words and actions be pleasing to You. And let the things I meditate and dwell on be acceptable to You. You are my Lord, my Rock, and my Redeemer. I love and praise You.

El Sali ... The God of My Strength; God, my Rock

Be exalted, O Lord, in Your strength; we will sing and praise Your power. Psalm 21:13

Prayer Response to Psalm 20

Mighty God and Father, I have an advantage over David in that I have access to Your entire Word. Your Word assures me that if I ask anything according to Your will, You hear me. I have personally experienced Your help in times of need. Your Word assures me that when I delight in You, You will give me the desires of my heart.

Father, keep me in that place of dependence and quiet rest in You, and let me delight in Who You are. Dear Lord, I praise and thank You for saving me and for never letting me go. I am secure in Jesus. There is no power in heaven or on earth that compares to You. You are God Almighty and my Everlasting Lord. I put my trust in You.

El Gibbor ... The Mighty God

Prayer Response to Psalm 21

Father, I praise You that my strength comes from You. I thank You for Your salvation and for hearing and answering my prayers. You have blessed me with eternal life and continue to bless me with good and perfect gifts that come from You. You give me every spiritual gift in the heavenly places. You give me joy and gladness and the fruit of the Spirit. I abide in sweet fellowship with You. Your love and kindness overwhelm me. You have been my stronghold and my Rock through the storms of life.

Father, You defend everyone who calls upon Your name. I cannot understand how so many people either deny You or hate You, but I am surrounded by them every day. Keep me steadfast and give me opportunities to be a witness for Jesus.

Father, I know that judgment is coming because Your Word continually warns us. Have mercy, Lord, on those who have rejected You, and continue to draw men and women and children to Jesus. I especially pray for my family and friends who do not know You. Show me what I need to do and give me the fortitude to obey.

Father, You are a loving and merciful God, while You are also a holy and just God. I praise You for Your strength and power. You are exalted above the heavens and the earth!

El Rachum ... The God of Compassion

All the ends of the earth will remember and turn to the Lord,
and all the families of the nations will worship before You.
Psalm 22:27

Prayer Response to Psalm 22

God of my salvation, Jesus cried out to You as He was separated from You on the cross. As He was dying and bearing the sins of a lost world, He felt as if You, His Father, had forsaken Him! I cannot begin to imagine that sense of separation. And thankfully, I do not have to. Jesus bore my sins on the cross. He shed His blood and faced separation from You so that I can be forgiven and stand before You just as if I had never sinned. Jesus paid the penalty for my sin, and I have accepted Your free gift of salvation. Because of that decision You have promised to never leave nor forsake me.

I praise You for that promise and for reminding me of Your eternal presence when life is difficult and You seem far away. I stand secure on that promise. We live in a very sinful world and life just is not fair. You warned us that in this life there will be tribulations. But You also encouraged us by reminding us that You have overcome the world. Help me to always remember that You are still on the throne, no matter what the circumstances are.

Enable me to commit my way to You and delight in You, and to always remember that You have already claimed victory. You are the One Who formed me in my mother's womb and You are the One Who drew me unto Yourself. Even when it seems like everyone and everything is against me, Lord, You are still with me. You are my helper, my strength, and deliverer. You see the afflictions of Your children, hear our cries, and You answer our prayers according to Your will. I praise and thank You for Your ever-abiding presence.

One day everyone will recognize Jesus as Lord. Peoples from every nation, tribe, and tongue will bow down and worship You. Meanwhile, we know that there are many who do not know You and it is up to me and everyone who does know You to live our lives in a way that is pleasing to You, and to pass on to the next generation the testimony of

Your greatness and the great salvation that is found in Jesus. You have provided the way for every generation to know You. Jesus said, "I am the way, and the truth, and the life; no one comes to the Father but through Me." (John 14:6) Thank You, Jesus, for saving me.

El Yeshuatenu ... The God of Our Salvation

The Lord is my shepherd, I shall not want. Psalm 23:1

Prayer Response to Psalm 23

Lord, I memorized this Psalm years ago, and it has been read at almost every funeral I have attended. What a comfort Your Word is to me every time I read it.

Lord, You truly are my Shepherd. You saw this little lost lamb and You rescued me out of the miry clay and have kept me in Your care ever since. As my Shepherd You provide my needs and so much more. You give me peace and rest when I need it. You restore my soul when I am in spiritual drought. You guide and direct my steps and keep me on the straight and narrow path. You do these things because I belong to You and You love me.

Even when I have walked through difficult times, You have encouraged, comforted, and calmed my fears. I am confident that when death comes, You will give me dying grace. I have witnessed how You have given dying grace to others and I trust You will do the same for me. You comfort me in all my afflictions.

Even when I am disciplined by You, it is done in love because I belong to You. Your intention is always restoration. You show me Your favor even when others are against me.

Father, my heart overflows with joy, knowing that I belong to You. I praise You for Your goodness to me and the loving-kindness that You continually pour out. Oh Father, keep me ever so close to You. I love You, Lord. Thank You for being my Good Shepherd.

El Shaddai ... The All-Sufficient God

The earth is the Lord's, and all it contains, the world, and those who dwell in it. Psalm 24:1

Prayer Response to Psalm 24

You, Lord, are Creator of heaven and earth, and everything belongs to You, including me. Father, You are more majestic and awesome than my mind can possibly comprehend. Because You are a holy God, You desire Your children to be holy and to be pure in heart.

The Bible, Your inspired Word, teaches me everything I need to know to live according to Your will. If I seek You with all my heart, You promise I will find You. Lord, it is my desire to continually seek You above all else, with all my heart. Continue the good work You began in me and help me to be honest and genuine before You. There is never a need to pretend because You know me better than I know myself.

I know I am sinful and my only righteousness is in Jesus. I have been purchased by the precious blood of the Lamb. I praise and thank You, Jesus, for Your great salvation. You are strong and mighty, the King of Glory and the Lord of Hosts. My hope is in You.

El Hakkavod ... The God of Glory

Lead me in Your truth and teach me, for You are the God of my salvation; for You I wait all the day. Psalm 25:5

Prayer Response to Psalm 25

I praise You, Lord, for another day that I can come into Your presence and lift my soul to You, to tell You that I love You and trust You.

Father, teach me Your ways and guide my steps. Help me to focus on You instead of people. You are the God of my salvation and I ask that You lead me into Your truth. Help me to wait upon You. You are loving and compassionate, and I thank You for the forgiveness of sin that I have in Christ. He shed His blood so that my sins could be washed clean. I am thankful that those sins I have confessed and repented of are forgiven and no longer remembered by You. They are as far as the east is to the west.

May I not take for granted Your mercy and grace. Give me a thankful heart and an obedient spirit. Your Word tells me that the fear of the Lord is the beginning of wisdom. Enable me to revere and honor You in the way You deserve. Keep my heart in tune with Yours and my eyes focused on Jesus.

I praise You for Your grace, comfort, and peace when I am facing struggles and feeling all alone. Thank You for encouraging me and strengthening me to overcome.

Father, I praise You that my life is in Your hands. You faithfully watch over me and keep me secure. How thankful I am that You hide me under Your wings.

Lord, keep me honest and pure as I wait for Jesus to return or until You take me home. You, oh Lord, are the God of Israel. Bless Your chosen people and reveal to the nation of Israel that Jesus is Messiah.

El Yisrael ... The God of Israel

Wait for the Lord; be strong and let your heart take courage; yes, wait for the Lord. Psalm 27:14

Prayer Response to Psalm 26

Gracious Father, I am thankful I can come to You completely justified because I come to You in the name of Jesus. Because I have placed my faith and trust in the finished work of Christ, I come before You in His righteousness.

Apart from Jesus, I would not be able to walk in Your ways, be honest, or sincere. Without Christ, I would not be able to overcome sinful actions and words that displease You. In fact, without Jesus I can do nothing. Because Jesus has changed my heart, I no longer desire the things of this world. You have given me a new desire: to be like Jesus. Father, when the doors of Your house are open, I look forward to fellowshipping with others who love and worship You. My heart overflows with thanksgiving for Your innumerable blessings. Thank You for Your grace and Your redemption. You have enabled me to stand secure, and I will continue to bless You and praise You. Thank You for Your amazing grace.

El Channun ... The Gracious God

Prayer Response to Psalm 27

Faithful God and Father, Jesus is the Light of the World. He is the Way, the Truth, and the Life. He is my Light and my Savior. There is never a reason that I should fear because You are much greater than any enemy I could possibly face.

Lord, You are my righteous defender, and my confidence is in You. You have guided and protected me all the days of my life. David longed to dwell in the house of the Lord, but I am so blessed that Jesus dwells in me. He never leaves nor forsakes me. He readily hears my cries for help and answers me. He even intercedes for me.

Father, You are so good to me. Continue to teach me Your ways and strengthen me. As I seek You, grant me the patience, Lord, to wait upon You. I praise You for Your faithfulness and for being patient with me.

El Hanne'eman ... The Faithful God

The Lord is my strength and my shield; my heart trusts in Him, and I am helped; therefore my heart exults, and with my song I shall thank Him. Psalm 28:7

Prayer Response to Psalm 28

Father, how grateful I am that You are always listening when I speak to You. When everything around me is crumbling and falling apart, You are my Rock and firm foundation. I cannot imagine what life would be without You.

Lord, I ask that You strengthen my heart and enable me to overcome the temptations of this world. Evil lurks everywhere and sin is so deceptive. Father, set me apart from those who do not know You and those who live selfishly and sinfully. But Lord, help me not to be judgmental, and to express to them Your love, pray for them, and point them to Jesus.

Father, I praise and thank You that You are my strength and my shield. You answer all my prayers and I trust You. Forgive me for the times that I doubt.

I thank You for my salvation and ask that You continue to draw others to Jesus. I pray especially for my family and others that I love. Enlighten their hearts, minds, and eyes to see their need for a Savior. Draw them to Jesus. Please, Lord, have mercy on their souls. Thank You for being my Shepherd. Reveal to others that You are the Good Shepherd Who lays down His life for His sheep. What a Savior!

El Yeshuatenu ... The God of Our Salvation

Prayer Response to Psalm 29

God, You are so awesome, and this Psalm reminds me that in the beginning You spoke all things into being. You are mighty and powerful! All of creation was created by Your spoken word! You alone are worthy of my worship and praise. How majestic and glorious You are! I see Your handiwork everywhere. You are the King of Kings and Lord of Lords.

Strengthen Your people, Lord, with Your might, and grant us Your peace. What an awesome God You are!

El Hannora ... The Awesome God

But as for me, I trust in You, O Lord, I say, You are my God.
Psalm 31:14

Prayer Response to Psalm 30

Great God and Heavenly Father, I cannot help but praise You for Who You are to me and all that You do for me! You are my God, my Lord, and my Heavenly Father. You hear me when I call out to You and heal me when I am physically and spiritually sick.

Lord, You chose me before the foundation of the earth and saved my soul from hell. It is You Who gives me life and it is You Who keeps my life. I praise Your holy name! And Lord, when I do sin and You must chastise me, I know You still love me. You do whatever is necessary to keep me close to You. You are a loving Father and Your anger is short-lived. Once I confess my sin, You graciously forgive. Our fellowship is restored and Your joy is renewed in my heart. You are so gracious and faithful, and my heart overflows with praise and thanksgiving.

El Haggadol ... The Great God

Prayer Response to Psalm 31

Dear Lord, no matter what is going on in my life, I am comforted to know that You are with me. You have seen my life from beginning to end and there are no surprises to You. Thank You for hearing and answering my prayers.

Father, when I am weak, You are strong. I depend on You to strengthen me and I depend on You to guide my steps. I love You and trust You and commit my life to You. I praise You for Your grace and mercy. I am so thankful that You forgive and restore me when I sin and fall out of fellowship with You.

Oh Father, You are so loving, kind, and good. I try to imagine all the wonderful things that You have prepared for me in heaven. Jesus is preparing a place for me and, although it is hard to imagine, I know it will be glorious! Thank You for Your salvation and the assurance that I am secure in Christ. You are so faithful. Please give me the grace to be strong, courageous, and faithful until You call me home. My hope is in Jesus.

El De'ot ... The God of Knowledge

How blessed is he whose transgression is forgiven, whose sin is covered! Psalm 32:1

Prayer Response to Psalm 32

Merciful Father, David was a man after Your heart and yet he sinned greatly. He experienced physical and mental distress when he tried to cover his sin, but David knew how to repent. As a result, he was able to experience Your forgiveness and restoration. Thank You for allowing me to learn from David's life, and help me, Father, to keep short accounts with You.

Sin affects us in so many ways. It separates us from You and we lose that sweet fellowship. Sin also affects us physically because we are no longer depending upon You for strength and vitality. Lord, I know there is no need to try and hide my sin because You are well aware of it. God, reveal to me the sin in my heart and, by Your grace, give me the courage and strength to confess and repent. Jesus said, "If we confess our sins, He is faithful and righteous to forgive us our sins and to cleanse us from all unrighteousness." (1 John 1:9) Thank You, Jesus, for bearing the penalty of my sin on the cross.

Father, You have been so faithful to me. You are my hiding place and You deliver me out of my troubles. You even give me songs to sing. You instruct and teach me through Your Word, and Your watchful eye is ever on me. Keep my heart tender and in tune with You. I praise You for Your love and kindness. My heart overflows with joy that I belong to You!

El Malei Rachamim ... All Merciful God

Blessed is the nation whose God is the Lord, the people whom He has chosen for His own inheritance. Psalm 33:12

Prayer Response to Psalm 33

I praise You, Lord, for another day. I praise You at different times, in different ways. Thank You for a voice with which I can praise You through words and songs. Thank You for the gift of music and the talent to play instruments which are used to bring honor and glory to You! How righteous, just, and faithful You are.

Your loving-kindness permeates the earth! Your power is so magnificent that the heavens and earth were created by Your spoken word! The waters of the oceans are all kept in place by Your power. You not only created everything but sustain it. All creatures great and small should stand in awe of You, for there is no one in heaven or earth like You.

Earthly leaders make decisions and plans, but You, Father, have the final Word. Your Word tells us that we make our plans, but You direct our steps. How grateful I am for that truth because You know all things and know what is best. My knowledge and the knowledge of others is limited. You have created each of us with a special plan and purpose for our lives. And You know what is required for those plans to be fulfilled. Too often, Lord, we depend upon our own strength or the strength of others instead of depending on You. Lord, forgive me when I trust anything or anyone instead of You.

Lord, I pray for our nation. We have lost sight of You. We have turned from You and have become extremely sinful. Our leaders are looking for answers in all the wrong things. Their wisdom is worldly and limited. Please, Lord, intervene. Send a revival to our nation. Raise up godly leaders who will depend upon You and will call upon You for wisdom, guidance, and discernment. Give us leaders who will unashamedly call upon You and follow You. We need Your blessing upon our nation.

Only You can change hearts. God, renew a righteous fear of You. Enlighten our hearts and minds to know that our hope is in You.

Father, my soul depends upon You and You are my hope, my help, and my shield. My trust is in You and I wait to see Your plan unfold. Have mercy on us, oh Lord. I praise You for Your loving-kindness that is everlasting.

El Hakkavod ... The God of Glory

The eyes of the Lord are toward the righteous and His ears are open to their cry. Psalm 34:15

Prayer Response to Psalm 34

I bless You, honor You, and magnify Your name. Father, enable me to brag on You whatever life's circumstances are. I confess it is much easier to praise You when life is good. Continue to remind me that You are the God of the good times and the bad. And even in the bad You promise to use it in my life for good.

Lord, this Psalm reminds me of the things that I can praise You for all the time. I praise You for answering all my prayers. When I am afraid, I call out to You and You replace fear with trust. You impart to me Your radiance and joy when I spend time with You. You provide for all my needs and deliver me out of my troubles. Your guardian angels surround me to protect and rescue me. You are my refuge all the time and Your arms are always open wide. You are my Rock and stronghold. You satisfy my life with Your goodness. Every good and perfect gift comes from You.

You give me life eternal and have determined the length of my days. You draw near to me when I am brokenhearted and I cry out to You. You comfort my heart and give me peace. When my spirit is crushed, You lift me up and replace despair with joy. You sent Jesus to die on the cross, to redeem my soul, and in Christ there is no condemnation. I can stand before You in Jesus, just as if I had never sinned. Hallelujah! Your watchful eye is always attentive to me, always leading, guiding, and directing my steps. How can I not praise You; You are so good to me!

El Roi ... The God Who Sees Me

Judge me, O Lord my God, according to Your righteousness.
Psalm 35:24

Prayer Response to Psalm 35

*A*lmighty God, please help me to understand, like David, that I need to depend on You to deal with those who oppose me. It is foolish for me to fight battles that I cannot control. Only You know the motives behind what people say and do and only You can change their hearts and minds.

Father, I know I belong to You; I strive to serve You and be the person that You have called me to be. Nevertheless, there will always be those who misjudge me, who misinterpret my words, and misrepresent me, and those who do not understand me. There will be those who want me to fail, and I may not ever know why. There will be those who dislike me for no good reason. And there may even be those who want to harm me. I am confident that You know the thoughts and motives of everyone, including me, and that You will judge righteously.

Lord, whatever enemy I face, I ask that You go before me and with me and that I will depend upon You for the right outcome. Give me the grace to not react with anger or bitterness. Help me to appropriate Your gifts of love and forgiveness. Jesus said that I should love my enemies and pray for those who spitefully use me. He also said that if someone strikes me on one cheek, to turn and offer the other cheek. Father, I cannot do any of these things apart from Your grace and power.

Lord, judge my heart and reveal to me my sin. I may be to blame and not even realize it. Your Word tells me that my heart is deceitful. Cleanse my heart and fill me with Your Holy Spirit. Lord, enable me to always respond with grace so that Your name will be honored. Forgive me when I fail. You are my righteousness. You are a righteous Judge.

El Tsaddik ... The Righteous God

Your lovingkindness, O Lord, extends to the heavens, Your faithfulness reaches to the skies. Psalm 36:5

Prayer Response to Psalm 36

Y ou, oh God, are holy and righteous in every way. Your holiness demands judgment against all sin. Your Word makes it clear that we are all sinners and the wages of sin is death. There is not a righteous man on earth who consistently does good and does not sin. Sin abounds in the hearts of mankind.

Father, so many people have absolutely no fear of You and do not seem to distinguish between good and evil. They are wicked and deceitful to the core and have set their course on the broad path of life. Despite this, You are a loving God, and Your love and gift of salvation extends to the vilest sinner.

When David wrote this Psalm, Jesus had not yet come. At the appointed time, Father, You sent Your Son Jesus to redeem sinners, to provide righteousness to everyone who places their faith and trust in Him. You saw our sinful state and provided for all of mankind a refuge, a Savior—the Way, the Truth, and the Life. "The Spirit and the bride say, 'Come.' Let the one who hears say, 'Come.' Let the one who is thirsty come, and the one who desires the water of life drink freely." (Revelation 22:17) I praise You for Jesus and for Your gift of salvation. Open the eyes of those who do not see Your great love and draw them to Jesus.

I praise You for the abundant life Jesus gives. Help others to see that there is more to life than self-centeredness and sinful pleasure. I praise You for Christ's righteousness that has been imputed, or ascribed, to me. No one can earn Your salvation; it is a gift that must be received. I praise You that You are my refuge and You protect me. I praise You for being my loving, gracious, kind, merciful Father. I praise You that I belong to Jesus and no one can snatch me out of His hand. Praise You, Jesus!

El Rachum ... The God of Compassion

Delight yourself in the Lord; and He will give you the desires of your heart. Psalm 37:4

Prayer Response to Psalm 37

Gracious and merciful God, You tell me not to worry about things but to pray about everything. That includes those who continue in their evil ways. Father, forgive me for the times that I do fret over the evil that is taking place in my family, our nation, and around the world. Help me to faithfully pray for the salvation of souls and to do my part in sharing the Gospel. Only Jesus can change people's hearts.

Lord, enable me to focus on Jesus. Help me to trust You and enable me to do what You have revealed is right and good. Help me to cultivate faithfulness and to delight in You so Your desires will be mine. Daily, enable me to commit my way to You, to rest in the righteousness of Jesus, and wait on You for guidance and direction. Grant me Your grace to not worry or get angry, but to walk humbly before You.

Father, there are times when it seems like evil has the advantage. It seems as if the people who reject You are more prosperous than those who love You. Those who follow You are persecuted all around the world. But Father, this world is temporary and eternity awaits us all. Jesus told us to expect tribulations, but that He has overcome the world. Have mercy on those who continue in their sin and reject Jesus. Draw them and reveal to them their need for Christ.

Lord, You sustain and bless me during the good and bad times. You establish my steps. Your hand is ever holding on; when I fall, You pick me up and, Lord, You actually delight in me! Amazing! I am never forsaken and I am preserved forever. Thank You, Jesus!

Father, grant me Your wisdom so that my speech will reflect You. Keep my love for Your Word strong and enable me to apply the things that You reveal to me. Keep me on the straight and narrow path and continue to teach me to wait on You. I praise You for Your salvation and the righteousness I have in Jesus. I praise and thank You for Your strength and that You abide in me. You are my refuge. I need You, Lord.

El Olam ... The Everlasting God

For I hope in You, O Lord; You will answer, O Lord my God.
Psalm 38:15

Prayer Response to Psalm 38

Righteous and merciful Father, I pray that You would keep me from sin. David has clearly described the effects of unconfessed sin in his life. I have witnessed it in the lives of others and have experienced it in my own life. Lord, I want to avoid the agony and despair that comes with disobedience. There have been times when I knew in my heart of hearts that I deserved Your chastisement and, yet, like David, I have appealed to Your mercy.

Father, sin leaves Your children with a feeling of emptiness as we find ourselves separated from You. There is a lingering sense that Your hand is pressing hard, with no relief. Physical weakness sets in and, sometimes, illness because the burden of sin is more than we can bear. The memory of the sin lingers on in our mind, day and night, and our hearts are crushed beneath the burden. Sin not only affects our well-being but our loved ones and friends. We are no longer pleasant to be around and those we love, pull away. We lack Your wisdom, discernment, guidance, and direction, and make foolish decisions because we are no longer dependent upon You. We know You are fully aware of our sin because You see and know all things; and yet we remain silent until we can take it no more and we confess our sin and seek Your forgiveness.

Oh God, help me avoid the separation from You and the anxiety that accompanies sin. Help me abide in You. Holy Spirit, continue to search my heart, reveal my sin, and give me the grace to confess and repent. Lord, help me keep short accounts with You. Father, You are loving and merciful and, like the father of the Prodigal Son, always waiting and ready to forgive. Thank You for Your measureless love, mercy, and grace. Thank You, Jesus, for saving my soul. I am eternally grateful.

El Malei Rachamim ... All Merciful God

Behold, You have made my days as handbreadths, and my lifetime as nothing in Your sight; surely every man at his best is a mere breath. Psalm 39:5

Prayer Response to Psalm 39

Gracious Lord, Your Word tells me that my speech should always be gracious and that I should be wise in my dealings with others. Because I am fleshly and weak, I fail in this area and I know I must depend upon You to guard my mouth and guide my steps. Change my heart because what is in my heart will eventually come out. Convict me of any prejudices, bad attitudes, and unforgiveness.

Life is so short, and it is my desire to let Your fruit of the Spirit flow through me. I want my life to look like Jesus in word and deed. I have such a long way to go! I know with my mind that this earth is not my home. Yet it is so easy to get caught up in thinking and acting like the world. Jesus warned us that this world is passing away. Lord, deliver me from all my sins so that I will not hurt You or others and I will not need to be disciplined.

Jesus is coming back to claim His bride and I want to be found faithful when He returns. Help me to number my days and to wisely redeem the time I have remaining. Life is so short. Keep me close to You until the end.

El Channun ... The Gracious God

I waited patiently for the Lord; and He inclined to me and heard my cry. Psalm 40:1

Prayer Response to Psalm 40

Oh Father, You are so patient with me, always watching and listening and waiting for me to call out to You. Help me to be more patient as I wait on You.

Thank You for lifting me out of the miry clay of sin and restoring my soul. You continually renew my heart with joy and praise and give me songs with which to praise You. You continue to strengthen me and firmly establish my steps. I pray that my life will be a witness to others as I place my trust in You.

There is no one in heaven or on earth like You. Your magnificent power is seen in all of creation. Your awesome works are too numerous to name; yet in all of creation, You love me and care about my needs. You reaffirm to me that You are not interested in my works or the sacrifices I make; You are interested in my heart.

You have placed within me a love for Your Word and a desire to do Your will. You have given me opportunities to share Your great love with those who know You and those who do not. I have been able to testify of Your faithfulness and my undeserved salvation. I attest that You are compassionate, loving, and kind. I share Your Word and how You speak to my heart. Father, I ask that You keep evil far from me and that I not be overcome by sin. May I continue to seek You, rejoice in You, glorify You, and always be grateful for Your salvation through Jesus. You are my deliverer.

El Hannora ... The Awesome God

As the deer pants for the water brooks, so my soul pants for You, O God. Psalm 42:1

Prayer Response to Psalm 41

Y ou are Alpha and Omega, the beginning and the end. You are my Everlasting Lord. Help me, Father, to be more compassionate and loving to those who are helpless and in need. Enable me to genuinely care for others like Jesus did, and does. Help me express the same goodness and kindness You have lavished on me.

You give me life and protect me from harm. You deliver me out of the struggles of life. You sustain me when I am sick and restore my health. You forgive my sins and heal my soul. You are my faithful friend even when all others turn away. You, Lord Jesus, are my advocate and my intercessor. You never leave me nor forsake me. How can I not praise You! Your grace is overwhelming.

El Channun ... The Gracious God

Prayer Response to Psalm 42

F ather, You created me to have fellowship with You, and You placed within my heart a need and a desire that only You can fill. Thank You for sending Jesus, and, Jesus, thank You for filling that void. I pray I will continue to possess that longing in my heart, to remain close to You. Continue to give me that deep down in the soul thirst for You.

David's enemies kept him on the run, and he was unable to meet in Your house of worship. How he longed to worship in Your house once again. It is obvious that David loved You and depended upon You for his strength, protection, and deliverance. David had the same inner struggle that I have from time to time. The circumstances of life can seem overwhelming, so I come to You to work through my struggles.

You always remind me of Your greatness, Your love and kindness, Your divine protection, and Your presence. You remind me that You are my Rock and my hope is in You. You remind me that my earthly life is short and the difficulties I face are temporary. They are nothing compared to the glory of eternity in heaven. Lord, how thankful I am that You have given me eternal life and Your Holy Spirit resides in me. He enables me to remember Your Word and points me back to Jesus. No matter what is going on in life, I have much to praise You for. I pray that my words, actions, thoughts, and even my countenance will reflect Christ. I love You, Lord.

El Roi ... The God Who Sees Me

For He knows the secrets of the heart. Psalm 44:21

Prayer Response to Psalm 43

*A*lmighty God and gracious Lord, as I look around and see what is going on in this country and around the world, I, too, cry out for mercy and deliverance. Sin abounds and people's hearts are deceitful. Injustice seems to be the norm, and those who have received Jesus as their personal Savior and Lord are persecuted around the world. I see the enemy of our souls blinding the hearts and minds of many, and some are oppressed.

Oh Father, You are greater than the enemy. You sent Jesus to show us the way. Remove the blinders and enable people to see You. Enable them to understand Your great love and reveal to them Your salvation that is available to them in Christ. Jesus is the hope of the world, and I praise You for Your forgiveness and saving grace.

El Tsaddik ... The Righteous God

Prayer Response to Psalm 44

*D*ear God of ages past, Your Word is filled with testimonies of how You lovingly guided and directed Your people. The sons of Korah remembered that it was You Who established the nation of Israel. You defeated their enemies and allowed them to enter the Promised Land. It was You alone and Your favor toward Israel that made them a great nation. But it was also You Who allowed defeat and allowed humiliation. It was You Who allowed the heathen nations to take Israel captive because of unconfessed sin. As a nation, Israel broke their covenant with You, and judgment came.

Father, I now remember how You have blessed our nation. For many years, our country had been the envy of the world because Your favor was upon us. The United States of America was founded upon godly principles and even on our coins is stamped "In God We Trust." Our motto is "One Nation Under God" and at one time we stood strong in that truth.

But Lord, we have turned away from those godly principles. As a nation, we no longer seek or trust You. We are sinning greatly, with no remorse or repentance, and we are reaping what we have sown. Like the sons of Korah, I ask that You, oh God, be merciful to us as a nation. Unless You intervene, unless You send a revival and our hearts turn back to You, our nation will be like the others that have abandoned You. How my heart aches to think this may happen. Father, please help us and redeem us, for the sake of Your loving-kindness.

El Malei Rachamim ... All Merciful God

I will cause Your name to be remembered in all generations;
therefore the peoples will give You thanks forever and ever.
Psalm 45:17

Prayer Response to Psalm 45

Eternal God and Father, only Jesus is the King of Kings and eternal God. Even when He became flesh, He was righteous, perfect, and sinless in every way. If He had not been, He would not have been the perfect sinless Lamb to take away my sin and the sins of the world. Every word from His mouth is gracious and Jesus Christ alone is the Mighty One, exuding splendor and majesty. Jesus is truth and He is meek and lowly of heart.

Lord Jesus, You are the Anointed One, the Messiah Who came to take away the sins of the world. One day every knee will bow and every tongue will confess that You are Lord. Meanwhile, Your children praise You and adore You and await Your return. Your kingdom is eternal, where only righteousness resides.

Thank You, Jesus, for dying for me and imparting to me Your righteousness. You have purchased me with Your precious shed blood, and I submit my life to You as my Lord. I rejoice that I am a child of the King. I pray that my life will be a testimony to the generations behind me, of what You mean to me. Give me many opportunities to share You with others, especially my family. You have prepared a place for me in heaven and I want my loved ones to join me there at their appointed time. Jesus, Your name is above all names. I give You praise and thanks.

El Olam ... The Everlasting God

Cease striving and know that I am God ... Psalm 46:10

Prayer Response to Psalm 46

Almighty God and Heavenly Father, I praise and thank You for Your ever-abiding presence. In good times as well as bad times You are always with me. In the difficulties of life, I run to You, my refuge. You impart to me Your strength, enabling me to face each challenge. Your grace has been sufficient for every need, even when I felt like I had reached the end.

Everything in this life changes, but You, oh Lord, are the same yesterday, today, and forever. There is never a reason to be fearful, because You are sovereign and You sustain the entire world. Whether my family or the whole world is falling apart, You are my stronghold, my solid Rock.

Thank You for Your Word and the testimonies of Your power and greatness throughout. But Lord, I also praise You for all the wonderful things You have done in my life. My past is a testament of Your goodness and faithfulness, and I am overwhelmed. Thank You for guiding and directing my life because there are so many things I do not understand. But that is okay because I know Jesus and He understands all things.

Continue to mold me and make me. Help me to cease all striving and to rest in the fact that You are God. You Who began a good work in me will complete it. You know all things, see all things, and are in absolute control of all things. I trust You, Lord. Increase my faith and trust in You. You alone are worthy of my praise.

El Sali ... The God of My Strength

Prayer Response to Psalm 47

You are the Lord Most High and King of all the earth. You are my Creator and sustainer and are worthy of praise. I praise You, Lord, with my heart and voice. I praise You with hymns and songs of praise. I praise You with the joy You have placed within me.

You are sovereign, whether man acknowledges it or not. You control all things, including those nations and leaders who reject You. Their power is limited, but You, oh God, are almighty, omnipotent, omniscient, and omnipresent. You reign high above the earth and exert Your power over the nations. You are highly exalted. Hallelujah!

El Elyon ... The Most High God

No man can by any means redeem his brother or give to God a ransom for him—For the redemption of his soul is costly, and he should cease trying forever— Psalm 49:7–8

Prayer Response to Psalm 48

Lord, there is no one in heaven and earth that compares with You. You are great and greatly to be praised. The earth and the galaxies beyond are Your handiwork and far greater than I can comprehend!

You chose the nation of Israel to be a light to the nations and established Jerusalem as the city of God. And yet Your people have never rendered You the praise You deserve, nor have they obeyed You.

Jehovah, Your name is too holy to speak. You are righteous in all Your judgments, and Your loving-kindness extends to all generations. I praise You that You are eternal God and that You guide and direct my life and will continue to do so until I die. My life is in Your hands.

El Echad ... The One God

Prayer Response to Psalm 49

God of my salvation, Your Word is clear that salvation is obtained only through faith in Jesus Christ. No amount of riches or works can buy it, even though redemption was extremely costly.

Forgive me, Lord, for placing too much emphasis on material wealth and earthly goods. Even the wealthiest man on earth cannot buy his way to heaven and, when he dies, none of it will go with him. Jesus said this world and everything in it is passing away, along with its lust. Everything that I accumulate in this life will be left to someone else and, honestly, it may end up with perfect strangers.

Father, I am eternally thankful for Jesus and for His shed blood that purchased my pardon at Calvary. I have been purchased with the precious blood of Christ. My sin debt cost Jesus His life. I praise You for such a great and powerful love. Because Jesus has redeemed my soul, I belong to You. Jesus is preparing a place for me in heaven and one day I will see Jesus face-to-face.

Oh Lord, I pray that those I love and those You place in my life will realize their need for Christ. Life is short and all that is in this life is temporary. Jesus alone gives eternal life. Thank You for saving my soul!

El Yeshuati ... The God of My Salvation

He who offers a sacrifice of thanksgiving honors Me ...
Psalm 50:23

Prayer Response to Psalm 50

Mighty God and Lord of my life, You created all of mankind in Your image so we can have fellowship with You and bring honor and glory to Your name with our lives. All of creation was deemed good until sin entered the picture. Sin caused man's fellowship with You to be broken and sin had to be dealt with. Even in the garden, an animal's blood was shed so that Adam and Eve's nakedness was covered. You provided that sacrifice and sin covering in the garden, and You have continued to pour out Your love and provide a way for man to be reconciled to You.

You made the covenant with Abraham, the nation of Israel, Your chosen people. You gave them so many promises, and their responsibility was obedience to You and Your Word. Time and time again they sinned and rebelled against You because their hearts were sinful. Outwardly they performed the necessary sacrifices, but You are not pleased with outward appearances.

You are always looking at our hearts. As a loving Father, You discipline those who belong to You because You are forever desiring restoration. Father, guard my heart. What is in there will eventually come to light. My desire is to be sincere and humble before You. Cleanse me and fill me to overflowing with the fruit of Your Spirit. Give me a grateful heart.

Father, I am so thankful that You never gave up on mankind. I am thankful that You loved this world enough to send Your Son Jesus to die on the cross, to be the propitiation for our sin. From the beginning You have required a blood sacrifice for sin and Jesus shed His lifeblood for mankind. I cannot fully understand it, but I am eternally grateful for my salvation through faith in Christ. He bore my sin so that I can stand before You, just as if I had never sinned. Thank You, Jesus.

Father, You have always been faithful to Your Word. I am trusting that You will complete the work You began in my life. I praise You for Your salvation and pray that my life will bring You honor and glory. May others see Jesus in me so they will be drawn to You.

El Gibbor ... The Mighty God

The sacrifices of God are a broken spirit; a broken and contrite heart, O God, You will not despise. Psalm 51:17

Prayer Response to Psalm 51

Gracious, loving, kind, compassionate, and forgiving Father, I humble myself before You, recognizing and acknowledging that I am a sinner and my heart is bent toward disobedience. I ask that You enable me to be more like David in the area of repentance. I pray that I would readily see and confess even the so-called little sins and fully understand that all sin offends You and that all sin is ultimately against You. Lord, I do not want anything to disrupt our fellowship, so I beg You to search out my heart and reveal to me those things that dishonor and grieve You. Then give me the grace to confess and repent.

Father, there have been times in my life when I felt like David. My sin blocked our fellowship together; my joy and strength were gone. But You readily reminded me that You know my bent and Jesus died on the cross so that my sins can be forgiven. Because of Jesus' shed blood, I can confess my sin, and He is faithful and just to forgive my sin and cleanse me from all unrighteousness. What a Savior! Forgiveness and cleansing come from You because You are compassionate, merciful, gracious, and forgiving.

Father, like David, I desire a clean heart and a renewed and steadfast spirit. Fill my heart to overflowing with Your Holy Spirit and restore the joy of Your salvation. Give to me a willing spirit. Unless my sins are forgiven and my heart is right with You, I am not able to teach others and be a witness for Christ. Father, keep me on the straight and narrow path and keep my heart humble before You.

El Malei Rachamim ... All Merciful God

God has looked down from heaven upon the sons of men to see if there is anyone who understands, who seeks after God. Psalm 53:2

Prayer Response to Psalm 52

*A*lmighty God and merciful Father, sin abounds everywhere! The whole world is in turmoil! I should not be surprised, because Your Word tells me that our hearts are deceitful above all else and desperately wicked. People all around seem to spew out hate and their actions are divisive and destructive. Stealing, looting, murder, and hateful speech have become the norm. The sad part is, they revel in it! Lying has replaced truth and it is difficult sometimes to discern the truth.

Oh Father, You sent Your Son to redeem us from such a life and yet most people reject Jesus. Holy Spirit, open their hearts and minds to see the difference that Jesus makes and draw them to a saving knowledge. Jesus is the Prince of Peace. Only Jesus can change a person's heart. Thank You for revealing to me Your gift of salvation, for giving to me a heart of flesh and the gift of Your indwelling Spirit. You are my refuge and a refuge to all who love and trust Christ.

Those who trust in their riches and goodness will one day face judgment. I am so thankful for Your great love and kindness. You have blessed my life and because of Jesus' shed blood, I will enjoy eternity with You.

El Emet ... The God of Truth

୕

Prayer Response to Psalm 53

*O*h Father, according to Your Word, there are many fools in this world because the multitudes refuse to acknowledge that You exist! That blows me away because I see Your hand in all of creation. Only You, Almighty God, could create this universe with such order and precision and hold it all together.

Yet, Lord, sin did enter the world and flawed mankind so that people do not understand nor seek You. Even those who acknowledge Your existence fail to submit to Your lordship and obey Your Word. There is no one who consistently does good. But You are merciful and provided a Savior so we can have restored fellowship with You, a holy and righteous God.

Jesus came to redeem sinners, yet Israel, Your chosen nation, rejected Him as Messiah. How thankful I am that Your mercy extended to all peoples and that all who call upon Jesus' name will be saved. Your Word tells us that in heaven there will be people from every tongue, tribe, and nation. What a glorious place heaven will be! Your salvation did come out of Zion. Thank You, Jesus.

El Yeshuatenu ... The God of Our Salvation

Cast your burden upon the Lord and He will sustain you; He will never allow the righteous to be shaken. Psalm 55:22

Prayer Response to Psalm 54

Oh God, how thankful I am that I can always call to You. You hear and answer my prayers according to Your perfect plan and will. In my times of distress and difficulties, You are the One I seek for help. You, Lord, are the One Who sustains me and prepares the way before me. You have been faithful to me all these years and You will remain faithful to the end. I love You, Lord. Help me be faithful to You.

El Hanne'eman ... The Faithful God

Prayer Response to Psalm 55

Oh Father, as I read this Psalm I can so relate to David. Life is filled with so many difficult circumstances and many times my troubles are overwhelming ... until I give them all to You. How thankful I am that You patiently listen to all my complaints and concerns and You understand me better than I understand myself. When I am restless, You give me peace.

There are times when I have been afraid and just wished that I could run away and hide. But instead of running away, I run to You. You are my only refuge and I know You are in control of all my circumstances. Nothing escapes Your attention.

Like David, sometimes my heartaches come from those I deeply love and care about. How painful that is. We expect our enemies to give us grief, but oh, how it hurts when it comes from loved ones. But even then I know that only You can bring about healing, reconciliation, and restoration.

Father, You are the same yesterday, today, and forever. You are the One constant in my life. I can always cast my burdens on You, knowing that You will sustain me and work in the hearts and lives of others. Thank You for Your grace and the promise that, as Your child, I am firmly in Your care. I can always trust You.

El Erekh Apayim avi ha-Tanchumim ...
The God of Patience and Consolation

When I am afraid, I will put my trust in You. Psalm 56:3

Prayer Response to Psalm 56

Gracious Lord, Your grace is sufficient for every need and I praise and thank You for Your unlimited grace showered upon me. I need Your grace daily as I constantly battle the enemy of my soul. Sometimes, Lord, I feel as though I am losing the battle, but then I remember to turn the circumstances of life to You. My spiritual enemy is always looking for ways to destroy me, but Jesus has already won the victory. You fully understand and are in complete control of every situation. You know my heart and I can trust You to work out the issues surrounding my life. You hear my every prayer and see every tear I shed. Nothing escapes Your attention.

I long for the day when Your children will live together in perfect harmony and unity. But until then, I praise You that I belong to You. Please, Lord, keep my feet on the narrow path and keep me from sin as I journey through this life. Help me walk in Your light and in the power of Your Spirit. I thank You for the shed blood of Jesus that continually cleanses me from all unrighteousness.

One day, sin will be no more and all who have received Christ as Lord and Savior will live in perfect unity with You. I love You, Lord, and look forward to the day when I see You face-to-face.

El-Channun ... The Gracious God

Prayer Response to Psalm 57

Gracious God and Heavenly Father, You are my refuge in times of need. Though emotions may overwhelm me at times, I know I am safe in Your care. You are for me, not against me, and that gives me peace.

Everything that happens is guided by Your loving hands. You accomplish things for me that I could never accomplish for myself. You cause all things to work together for my good. I praise You for Your guidance and protection. I praise You for Your truth and Your great love and kindness that You freely bestow on me daily.

Thank You, Jesus, for being my merciful high priest. You faithfully intercede on my behalf daily. Lord, You are highly exalted and Your glory is evident throughout the heavens and the earth. Keep my heart steadfast in You and enable me to be a faithful witness to all people. I praise You, Lord!

El Haggadol ... The Great God

Surely there is a God who judges on earth! Psalm 58:1

Prayer Response to Psalm 58

Righteous and Holy Father, You are indeed loving, patient, forgiving, and kind. And I must never forget that You are also holy and just.

I am a sinner by nature and my heart is corrupt. In fact, all of mankind is in a fallen state and that is why there is no justice on this earth. Violence, wickedness, and lying are clearly the results of life apart from Your saving grace.

You are loving and merciful and have provided the way for all to be redeemed. You sent Your Son Jesus to give His life as a ransom for our souls. He shed His blood so that man can be forgiven his sins and have his sinful nature changed.

Because I have placed my faith and trust in Jesus, I have become a new creation, and I praise and thank You for what You are working in my life. Continue to mold me and make me more like Him.

Have mercy on those who continue to reject Christ. Open their hearts and minds, reveal to them their need, and draw them to Jesus before it is too late.

Jesus, You are coming back to this earth and this time You are coming to judge those who have rejected Your gift of salvation.

Father, I am aware that the only righteousness I have is in Jesus. How thankful I am that I will not face Your judgment because Jesus already bore it for me on the cross. I can look forward to eternity in heaven with my Savior. Thank You for Your free gift of eternal life.

El Tsaddik ... The Righteous God

But as for me, I shall sing of Your strength; yes, I shall joyfully sing of Your lovingkindness in the morning, for You have been my stronghold and a refuge in the day of my distress. Psalm 59:16

Prayer Response to Psalm 59

All-powerful and merciful God, with each day that passes I become more and more aware of the spiritual enemy that I face. I realize I am no match and I seek Your deliverance from his schemes.

This Psalm reminds me of Who You are and Your character. You are my deliverer. You are Almighty God, and all the forces of hell are no match for You. I am secure in You because I belong to You. I claim Your promise that You will never leave me nor forsake me. You are faithful. Jesus bought me with His precious blood, and no one can snatch me out of His hand. You are my mighty defender and stronghold. You keep me safe.

I am the recipient of Your loving-kindness which is showered upon me all the days of my life. You are my loving Father. Each day that I awake, Your mercies are new. You are a God of mercy. You are all-powerful. There is no one like You; no one compares to You.

There is no need to fear any enemy because You are my shield. You protect me from the enemy's fiery darts. I am weak, Lord, but You are strong. Because You are my refuge, I can run to You and know that I am safe. You alone sustain my life. You are my defense; I need no other.

You are completely sovereign and judge all things with perfect righteousness. I can trust You because You are trustworthy. In Your providence, You have guided and directed my life and will continue to do so until You call me home. You are my hope, my all in all.

El Shaddai ... The All-Sufficient God

Through God we shall do valiantly, and it is He who will tread down our adversaries. Psalm 60:12

Prayer Response to Psalm 60

Holy and sovereign Lord, I am incapable of fully understanding just how holy You are because everything in this world is tainted with sin. But I know from Your Word that sin is detestable to You and sin must be judged.

David understood that Your favor required obedience and disobedience resulted in judgment. David knew it was You Who won the battles, and he knew the importance of remaining in a right relationship with You.

Because man is sinful and never could maintain the original covenant You made with Abraham, You sent Jesus into this world to be the propitiation for sin. He was the sinless and perfect sacrifice Who bore the judgment of my sin and the sins of the world so that we do not have to experience Your wrath. Oh, You are still holy and still hate sin, but You provided the ultimate and final sacrifice sufficient to cleanse us from all sins.

Thank You, Jesus, for sacrificing Your life for mine. Thank You for Your forgiveness of sin and victory over sin. But when I do sin, You promise that if I will confess my sin to You, my sin will be forgiven and You will cleanse me from my unrighteousness. Help me to never take Your grace for granted or abuse it in any way. Keep my heart in tune with Yours.

You are sovereign, and I am completely dependent upon You for life and breath. I am dependent upon You for salvation, strength, love, joy, peace, patience, and the list goes on. I praise You that You are my Heavenly Father and my victory is in You. Every good and perfect gift is from You. Thank You, Lord.

El Hakkadosh ... The Holy God

Trust in Him at all times, O people; pour out your heart before Him; God is a refuge for us. Psalm 62:8

Prayer Response to Psalm 61

Oh Father, I praise and thank You that You hear my prayers. When my heart is faint and weak, I need Your help. I know You are ever present.

Thank You for Jesus, Who is indeed my Rock, refuge, tower of strength, and shelter in the midst of every circumstance of life. In Him, I experience safety, peace, and comfort. Thank You for drawing me to Jesus and allowing me to share a glorious inheritance with those who love and reverence Him. Help me to abide in You and to love, serve, and obey You.

I praise You for Your mercy and kindness. I thank You for Your eternal Word that renews my mind and transforms my life. Thank You for sustaining my soul. May I forever praise Your name!

El Chaiyai ... The God of My Life

Prayer Response to Psalm 62

Dear Lord, You alone are my Rock and my salvation. In all areas of my life, enable me to trust Your will and Your wisdom and to surrender my will to Yours.

By Your providence, You guide and direct my steps, and by Your grace, You support and sustain me. Strengthen me and help me to prayerfully wait upon You with expectation. If You are for me, who can be against me? Man can only do what You allow. And You cause all things to work together for my good. You are my refuge, my place of safety. When I am doubtful and fearful, You encourage and strengthen me.

I praise You for Your Word and for all the many promises that are mine to claim. You, oh God, are powerful, merciful, kind, and just. Keep my eyes on You and not the things of this world, because this world and all that is in it is passing away. My hope is in You.

El Roi ... The God Who Sees Me

Because Your lovingkindness is better than life, my lips will praise You. Psalm 63:3

Prayer Response to Psalm 63

My God and Heavenly Father, my soul and heart long for You, Lord, because this world is like a dry and barren desert. This world cannot give peace, joy, comfort, and salvation. Only You can satisfy the deep needs of my heart and soul.

I continually seek You, for I have witnessed Your power and glory and will one day experience the joys of heaven with You. How precious is Your loving-kindness toward me, which will extend far beyond this temporal life!

Oh Father, it is easy to praise You when all is well. I ask that You give me the grace to praise You during times of affliction and turmoil. You are a merciful God Who comforts and supports me and gives me joy even in times of trouble. It is Your right hand that upholds me. If it were not for You, I would falter and fail.

Keep me humble before You and help me to always seek and love You. Let my enjoyment and satisfaction come from You and may You be my all in all.

El Echad ... The One God

Prayer Response to Psalm 64

I praise You, Lord, that You are always present and that You listen intently to my every prayer.

Like David, I, too, have circumstances and things in my life which I dread. Sometimes I am fearful. In those times I ask You to deliver me from those emotions and enable me to trust You. I look to You for strength and deliverance.

David had enemies who wanted to kill him. They were saying and doing things secretly, of which David had no control. Lord, there may be those who dislike me and say things to discredit me. There may be those who really hate or dislike me and wish to hurt me. I cannot control those situations, but I can trust that You will protect me and deliver me from evil.

Only You judge with perfect vision and righteousness. Only You know what resides in the heart of every person. I know You will always do what is right for me as well as my enemies. Jesus said I am to love my enemies and pray for those who persecute me. Holy Spirit, I need You to do that through me because I am not able.

How grateful I am that You are my refuge. I praise You for Who You are and all the marvelous things You do.

El De'ot ... The God of Knowledge

By awesome deeds You answer us in righteousness, O God of our salvation ... Psalm 65:5

Prayer Response to Psalm 65

Glorious and mighty God, You are worthy of praise from all of heaven and earth, and especially from Your chosen people.

Lord, I praise You for hearing my prayers and answering them as I come to You in the name of Jesus. I praise You that You loved me even as a sinner and provided for my salvation. You sent Jesus to die on the cross so that my sins are forgiven and I am at peace with You. Thank You for the restored fellowship that we share. Jesus satisfies the deep longings in my soul and He protects and sustains me. I am truly blessed. Keep me humble before You and give me a heart of thanksgiving.

By Your strength the mountains are established, and by Your power the ocean is contained and the seas calmed. That same strength and power are what keep me. I am amazed each day as the sun rises in the east and sets in the west, just as You ordained it. You are the One Who blesses the earth with water and grain. Your goodness and mercy are evident everywhere.

Thank You, Lord, for not giving me what I deserve, but for Your grace that meets my needs. What an awesome Father You are!

El Gibbor ... The Mighty God

God be gracious to us and bless us, and cause His face to shine upon us— Psalm 67:1

Prayer Response to Psalm 66

*A*wesome God, the psalmist calls upon me and the entire earth to shout and sing praises to You. Help me be faithful in testifying to others of all the wonderful things You have done in and through my life. Help me make a joyful noise, sing with pleasure, be open and public, and never be ashamed of Jesus. I praise and thank You for Jesus and the difference He has made in my life. Let my life bring honor and glory to You.

As Your children praise You, may it cause others to join in praise. Allow me to remind others that Your power and greatness are visible in all of creation and You are worthy of all praise. Your works declare Your wisdom, power, and faithfulness. You are the sovereign Almighty God Who keeps watch over all nations, and those who rule can only do what You allow. One day, everyone will bestow upon You the praise You rightfully deserve.

It is You, Father, Who gives me life, both physical and spiritual, and it is You Who sustains me. You protect me and You chasten me. When difficulties come, remind me that You are refining my life and molding me to be more like Your Son Jesus.

Lord, I ask that You guard my heart and keep me from sin. Sin breaks our fellowship and blocks my prayers. I praise and thank You for the forgiveness I have in Jesus. I praise You for Your loving-kindness, for Your many promises, and for hearing and answering my prayers. I love You, Lord.

El-Hannora ... The Awesome God

Prayer Response to Psalm 67

Gracious God and Father, where would I be without Your grace and undeserved blessing? I shudder to think! Thank You for revealing to me Who You are and revealing my need for a Savior. Thank You for Jesus and the magnificent salvation He gives to all who believe and receive. Reveal to all nations Your great love and open their eyes to see their need for Christ. Use me, Lord, to get Your message to a lost world.

Father, everyone is blessed by You to some measure. You cause the sun to shine on the righteous and the unrighteous, and You allow the earth to produce food and other resources for our needs. Open the eyes of those who fail to see that You are the giver of all good gifts. I praise You for Your goodness to all mankind.

El-Channun ... The Gracious God

The God of Israel Himself gives strength and power to the people. Blessed be God! Psalm 68:35

Prayer Response to Psalm 68

God Almighty and Lord of all, You reign over all creation, even those who reject and oppose You. Jesus told us that those who are not for You are against You. Forgive them and open their eyes to see their sinfulness, and draw them to Jesus. Help all to see that in comparison to Your greatness, we are insignificant.

I know that apart from You there is no real joy and eternal prosperity is found in a right relationship with You. You are compassionate and merciful to all. You care for the afflicted and oppressed and are Father to the fatherless. To all sinners You have provided salvation through faith in Your Son Jesus. You call all people unto salvation, but it is up to each person to accept it. Thank You for saving me, adopting me into Your family, and blessing my life.

David frequently recalled the past and the numerous ways You poured out Your mercy and blessings on Israel and on him personally. David recalled how Your presence was always with them, guiding and directing their path. He remembered Your goodness as You provided for their every need. He recounted how You protected them and gave them victory over their enemies.

I, too, remember my past and recall Your mighty hand leading, guiding, and directing my life. I have experienced Your salvation, provision, protection, and victories in Christ, and Your ever-abiding presence is precious to me. Remembering all the ways You have dealt with me in the past gives me strength for today and hope for tomorrow. You never change. You are the same yesterday, today, and forever.

As I read Your Word, You continually reveal Your love, compassion, grace, and mercy. And You also reveal Your holiness, justice, strength, and majesty. Thank You for Your continued strength. You are awesome. Praise be to You!

El ... God

May those who seek You not be dishonored through me, O God of Israel ... Psalm 69:6

Prayer Response to Psalm 69

Omniscient God and Father, David was in deep despair and desired relief from his suffering. I am so grateful that I never have to pretend with You. You are the One I can fully pour out my heart to and know beyond a doubt You already know and understand. Help me to always be honest and transparent with You. I also know that nothing is happening in my life that You did not allow and that You promise to cause all things to work together for my good. Only You have the answer regarding every situation.

David was hated without cause and constantly faced false accusations. His heart was broken, with no one to comfort him but You. Jesus was also falsely accused, rejected, and hated by His own people.

Forgive me for ever thinking that life will be different for me, for no servant is greater than his Master. Jesus and David were both misjudged and hated for following Your will. I pray that people will not judge or dislike me because of wrongdoing; however, that would be justified. But if they dislike me because I love and obey You, praise the Lord! I pray that my life will not dishonor You but will bring You honor and glory.

David had friends and relatives who were disloyal to him, and Jesus' disciples all forsook Him. It really hurts when those we care about turn us away. The bottom line is You are the only One I can fully trust. You judge all things and all people with perfect righteousness. May I be like David and Jesus and come to You in prayer about all things. You are loving, kind, good, and compassionate, and I long to stay close to You.

Father, David asked that You judge his wrongdoers, but Jesus told us to pray for our enemies. Give me Your grace to do just that.

Oh Father, You hear my cries and You promise to revive my heart as I seek You. I give You praise that You have saved my soul. I have a home in heaven and will one day reside there. Thank You, Jesus, for redeeming me and thank You, Father, that You are sovereign and nothing escapes Your watchful eye.

El Elyon ... The Most High God

*For You are my hope; O Lord God, You are my confidence
from my youth. By You I have been sustained from my birth ...
Psalm 71:5–6*

Prayer Response to Psalm 70

Oh Father, how grateful I am that You are ever present and always watching and listening. In my times of need, no matter how big or small, You are with me.

Thankfully, no one is seeking to kill me, but I am aware of those who say things about me that hurt. Father, please give me the grace to respond in love, and that I trust You to deal with their hearts.

I rejoice in the fact that I belong to You and You will never leave me nor forsake me. Friends come and go, but I can always rely on You. Thank You for being my helper and deliverer, my all in all.

El Shaddai ... The All-Sufficient God

Prayer Response to Psalm 71

Sovereign Lord, this Psalm reminds me once again of all that You mean to me. In times of distress and trouble, You are my refuge. Time and time again You have been my deliverer and rescued me from difficult situations. You have provided for my salvation in Jesus and You always hear my prayers. You are the solid Rock on which I stand. You never change and Your Word is eternal. You are my fortress when I need shelter and protection from the storms of life. Oh God, You are my hope for the future and the only confidence I have for the present.

You set me apart before the foundation of the earth. You have called me, saved me, and are consecrating me. It is You Who sustains me. I praise and thank You for Who You are and that I belong to You.

Your Word promises that You will not forsake me in my old age. You will never leave me nor forsake me, even when I am feeble and unable to do anything. I pray that You will enable me to witness to others regarding Your goodness and share the Good News of Jesus for as long as I am able. You offer salvation to all who will put their faith and trust in Your Son Jesus. What a glorious gift!

You are a holy and righteous God, and You are merciful and gracious. Thank You, Jesus, for imputing to me Your righteousness. This is such a sinful world, with many troubles and distresses. But thankfully, I never face anything without You. You provide comfort and strength. You revive my heart and have redeemed my soul. My heart praises You each and every day. Thank You for being my Heavenly Father, Savior, and Lord.

El Elyon ... The Most High God

Blessed be the Lord God, the God of Israel, who alone works wonders. Psalm 72:18

Prayer Response to Psalm 72

All wise and righteous Lord, Solomon understood his limited wisdom and ability to lead the nation of Israel. So he turned to You and asked You to enable him to be a righteous king. Solomon desired justice for the needy and afflicted and those who were oppressed. He longed for peace in a land where the righteous would flourish and be blessed.

Oh Father, if only our world leaders today would know You and cry out to You for Your wisdom, discernment, and guidance! I can only imagine how different our world would be. I pray that You will open the eyes of those who lead and enlighten their hearts so they will see You as King of Kings and Lord of Lords. I know when Jesus returns, that will happen.

Solomon's reign was temporary, but Jesus' reign will be for eternity. Only Jesus will reign with perfect righteousness. All kings and nations will bow before Him and every tongue confess that He is Lord. He will have compassion on the poor and needy and will deliver them. He will rescue those who are oppressed and are the victims of violence. Righteousness will flourish and there will be peace.

Until that time, I pray that You will pour out Your mercy on all people and pour out Your Spirit. Open blinded eyes that they may see You. Open my eyes and those of all who know You, to see others as You do. Help us to be merciful to those whom You put in our path and give us opportunities to share the love of Jesus. Help me, Father, to look like Jesus in a lost and dying world. I am Your hands, feet, and mouthpiece. Enable me to be faithful.

Father, I long for the day when sin is no more; when justice and peace reign, Your blessings abound and Your glory is evident to all. You are God Almighty, the God of Israel. You are my God and there is no other. I praise You for Who You are.

El Haggadol ... The Great God

*Whom have I in heaven but You? And besides You, I desire
nothing on earth. Psalm 73:25*

Prayer Response to Psalm 73

Dear righteous and just God, please deliver me from any
temptation to envy others, and especially those who do not
know You. Keep my heart and mind on eternal things and not
on the things of this world. This world and all its lust are passing away.
Remind me frequently of Your goodness; keep my feet from stumbling
and keep my heart from envy and pride.

Father, only You see and know all things, and appearances can be
deceptive. Only You know what is going on in the depths of each
person's heart. Sometimes it does appear that the wicked have it easier
than the righteous, but then I am reminded of Your goodness to all.

It is Your kindness, tolerance, and patience that lead people to
repentance. I am thankful that it is not Your will for any to perish. You
have shown great kindness and goodness toward me, and You have
drawn me to Jesus and revealed to me my need for salvation. Please do
that for my loved ones who have not believed and received Jesus.

Father, help me to dwell on Your love for me and Your ever-abiding
presence. Thank You for always guiding and directing my life and
keeping me safe. There is no one like You on earth or in heaven. I am
thankful You never leave me.

My earthly body is aging and my mind is not what it used to be, but
You are still the strength of my heart. How thankful I am that nothing
and no one can snatch me out of Your hand. You are my refuge. Please
give me many opportunities to share with others how much You mean
to me.

El Tsaddik ... The Righteous God

Arise, O God, and plead Your own cause ... Psalm 74:22

Prayer Response to Psalm 74

Merciful Father, how grateful I am that I can appeal to You on the basis that You are loving and merciful. Like the psalmist, there have been times in my personal life when things seemed bleak and I have wondered what was going on. There were times when it appeared that You had hidden Yourself from me. And yet I knew, and still know, that You never leave me and the circumstances of life are controlled by You. Because You are my Heavenly Father, I know that in Your time and Your way, Your will is going to be accomplished in my life. I belong to You.

As I look at our nation, it appears that You have hidden Yourself from us and the enemy of our souls is winning the battle. However, I know You are still sovereign, and Satan, along with all the forces of hell, can only do as much as You allow. In my personal life as well as nationally, I seek You and ask that You intervene.

Asaph seems to be describing the destruction of the temple and all that was sacred to him. He cried out to You to avenge the enemy and for deliverance. Father, today we are seeing similar things happening right here in our own country. I know that our nation has turned away from You and we are reaping what we have sown. Freedoms are being lost and what used to be wrong is now deemed right. Greed, murder, and lawlessness seem to prevail. Yet I still ask that You be merciful and gracious to our nation and that You protect Your children during these times. Like Asaph, I can look back and see the mighty things You have done in the past, and that inspires hope for the days ahead. You are the same yesterday, today, and forever.

Father, help me and all Your children to be shining lights in this dark world. May our lives point people to Jesus and help us to be faithful and bold in sharing the Gospel. Jesus is the hope of the world. Jesus told us to expect tribulations; however, He also told us to be encouraged because He has overcome the world. Keep reminding me that I am more than a conqueror in Christ. I praise You that You are Lord in every situation.

El Malei Rachamim ... All Merciful God

*We give thanks to You, O God, we give thanks, for Your name
is near; men declare Your wondrous works. Psalm 75:1*

Prayer Response to Psalm 75

Creator and sovereign God, I praise and give thanks to You for Who You are and all Your magnificent works. You established the earth, set all the boundaries, and created all that I see and cannot see. You continue to sustain it all. You, oh Lord, are the potter, and I am the clay. You are holy and righteous, and all Your judgments are right. Who am I to ever question Your ways?!

There are many powerful people in our world today who do not know You. They are selfish and greedy and willing to do anything in order to advance their careers and agendas. I know that You are Almighty God, and You are still on the throne as King of Kings and Lord of Lords. These people can only go as far as You allow. As Your child, I ask You to help me focus on Jesus and to seek and serve You. I continue to pray for those who abuse their power and I must leave the outcome totally in Your hands. Only You can change people.

Until Jesus returns, there will be a continual battle between evil and righteousness. Help me not to be afraid but to trust You. I praise You, Jesus, that You have already won the battle. Righteousness will prevail.

El Tsaddik ... The Righteous God

Prayer Response to Psalm 76

Great and mighty God, so many people in the world do not know You nor acknowledge Your name. However, You continuously reveal Yourself to me and others, Your power and majesty, and we praise You for Your greatness and Your goodness. Your dwelling place is now in the hearts of those who believe and trust You. Our bodies are the temples of the Holy Spirit.

As in the days of old, our enemies are no match for You, even the enemy of our soul. Thank You for Jesus, my righteous defender and Redeemer Who has already obtained the final victory. There is no power in heaven or on earth that can compare to You, so there is no need to fear.

By Your Word alone the earth was created, and by Your Word our enemies are defeated. Your Word, the Bible, reveals that the fear of man is a snare and the fear of You is the beginning of wisdom. I am sheltered in Jesus and I have no need to fear Your righteous anger. How thankful I am that Jesus already bore my judgment at Calvary.

I do not fully understand so many things, but I know that all things are designed to bring You the honor and glory You deserve, even the wrath of man. Your Word is jam-packed with promises and You are faithful to keep each of them. You deserve a faithful people, and I pray that I, for one, will remain faithful to You. Please forgive me when I fail.

I rejoice that I am Your child and that Your watchful eye is ever upon me. I thank You that I do not fight the battles in this life alone. You are my defender and Lord of Hosts.

El Gibbor ... The Mighty God

You have by Your power redeemed Your people, ...
Psalm 77:15

Prayer Response to Psalm 77

God of love, mercy, and grace, thank You for Your patience with me and all Your children in our fears, doubts, and sorrows. Over and over Your Word indicates that we live in a sinful and cursed world, and in this life there will be many trials and tribulations. Thankfully, we do not need to face our difficulties alone. Your Word reminds me that Jesus cares for me and that I am to bring all my concerns to Him because He cares about me.

Forgive me for the times that I am overwhelmed by my circumstances and I am not fully submitting and trusting You. Asaph was obviously overwhelmed, not at peace, and could not be comforted. He remembered better days, and that caused him to think that You had withdrawn Your favor, love, mercy, and grace. Meditating on Who You are and the mighty things You have done can bring things back into perspective.

Your Word also reminds me to seek You with all my heart, simply spending time with You and pouring out my soul. Even when You seem distant You are still with me. Your Word promises that You will never leave me. In times of trouble, help me remember Your unchanging character, Your glorious promises, and Your mighty works. Just as You provided for, guided, and protected Israel, You have done the same for me. Remind me of Your great love and care.

Israel was Your chosen nation and, by Your grace, I am Your chosen child. Before the foundation of the world, You chose me to do good things. You strengthened Israel and You continually strengthen me. Your strength is made perfect in my weakness. You redeemed Israel and You have redeemed me. I am redeemed by the precious blood of Jesus and nothing or no one can snatch me out of His hand. Forgive me for ever doubting You. There really is no need in ever being discouraged!

El Erekh Apayim avi ha-Tanchumim ...
The God of Patience and Consolation

And they remembered that God was their rock, and the Most High God their Redeemer. Psalm 78:35

Prayer Response to Psalm 78

Ancient of Days, You are from everlasting to everlasting, the same yesterday, today, and forever. You established Your covenant with the children of Israel and established Your commandments and laws for them to obey. They witnessed Your great miraculous power and experienced Your care, goodness, and favor over and over. You asked them not to forget Your mighty deeds, to keep Your commandments, and to put their trust and confidence in You. You also told them to be sure and pass all of this on to the next generation.

Lord, help me, as a parent and grandparent, to be faithful in setting a godly example. Help me to be obedient to Your Word and to be faithful in speaking to my children and grandchildren often about Your mercy as well as Your judgment. You are a loving and forgiving God, but You are also holy and hate sin. Sin separates us from You and sin must be punished.

You established a new covenant when Jesus came. Thank You for sending Jesus into the world as a perfect and final sacrifice for sin. You understand our sinful nature and You loved us enough that You gave Your Son as a sacrifice for my sin and the sins of the world. Through Jesus I have forgiveness of sin, power over sin, and the promise of eternal life. Help me to be faithful in sharing the Good News of Jesus because there is no other name in heaven or earth by which we can be saved.

In a world where so many have left You out, it is crucial that the next generation knows Jesus and obeys Him. Israel was unfaithful to You. Despite all the miracles You performed on their behalf, they forgot Your faithfulness and rebelled against You. When judgment came because of their sin, they cried out to You, and in Your mercy You forgave their sins. They went through this cycle many times. You restrained Your anger and remembered their frailty.

Father, I pray that You will forgive my sins, cleanse my heart, and renew my spirit. I confess the multitude of sins of our nation and I pray that all Your people will humble themselves and seek You. Forgive us for forgetting You. Without Your favor no nation is great. You have blessed us like You did with Israel as they entered Canaan. And, like Israel, we failed to remember that every good and perfect gift comes from You. Even when You send warnings to get our attention, we harden our hearts instead of turning back to You. Oh Father, how patient You are with us. Yet I know that You will not always strive with us. Have mercy on us, oh Lord.

El Malei Rachamim ... All Merciful God

*Help us, O God of our salvation, for the glory of Your name;
and deliver us and forgive our sins for Your name's sake.
Psalm 79:9*

Prayer Response to Psalm 79

God of our salvation, again and again Your chosen people, the nation of Israel, sinned against You. Each time they turned away from You, judgment came upon them and You used the godless nations to execute Your judgment. At some point they would confess their sin and repent. They would cry out to You for mercy. As I pray for our nation, we, too, have become a reproach to the world because of our sin. It appears that You have withdrawn Your favor and, like Asaph, I appeal to Your mercy and grace on behalf of our country. Like Asaph, I ask for forgiveness for the countless sins of our nation. Violence, hatred, and lawlessness abound, and we are reaping what we have sown. We do not deserve mercy, but I ask that You deliver us for Your name's sake.

Lord, our nation was founded upon godly principles by people who loved and trusted You, and Your favor was upon us. We were blessed by You and, in turn, our nation was a blessing to others. That is no longer true. Slowly but surely, we have forsaken You and Your commandments. Father, I pray that, as a nation, we will return to You and once again realize it is You Who makes us great. Apart from You, we are no different than any other nation.

I pray for our national leaders and ask that You convict their hearts of sin, righteousness, and judgment. I ask that You intervene on behalf of our country, that You pour out Your Spirit and revive us as a nation. Enable us to once again live as a nation that really does trust You, and help us to be a shining light to the world.

I acknowledge that You are sovereign and that You judge with perfect righteousness. I also acknowledge that You have a will and plan and, as Your child, I submit to You and trust You, no matter what the outcome. I praise You that You are all-powerful and You watch over Your children. Help me to be faithful in sharing Your goodness with future generations.

El Yeshuatenu ... The God of Our Salvation

O God, restore us and cause Your face to shine upon us, and we will be saved. Psalm 80:3

Prayer Response to Psalm 80

Shepherd of Israel, my Shepherd, as Asaph prayed for the restoration of Israel, I pray for the restoration of our nation. There is no question that our nation has sinned against You greatly. Hate, murder, pride, greed, materialism, selfishness, pornography, immorality, and theft are just a few sins, and the list goes on. The godly principles that our nation was founded upon are no longer considered. In God We Trust is a quote, but not a reality, and many want to remove it altogether. We are truly a nation that has rebelled against You.

Again and again, Israel would repeat the cycle of sinning and turning from You, until judgment came. They would cry out in their judgment, confess their sins, and repent. Each time, You forgave their sins and restored their nation. Unfortunately, their memory would lapse and the cycle would start all over again. What a patient Father!

I ask that You cause Your face to shine upon the United States once again and that You will save us from ourselves. I appeal to Your mercy since we certainly do not deserve it. Oh God, send a revival in our nation so that we will once again call upon Your grace and power. Help us, as a nation, to see that without You we are no different than any other. Turn our hearts toward Jesus. He came to this world and sacrificed Himself that we might have forgiveness of sin, an abundant life, and eternal life. There is salvation in no other.

We are all sinners in need of a Savior, and Jesus is the Way, the Truth, and the Life. In Jesus we become new creations; old things are replaced with new. Only Jesus can change the hearts of men and women. Please, Father, awaken us, revive us, and restore us before it is too late.

As Your child, I thank You for Your promises and the assurance that I belong to You. You will never leave me, and You will cause all things to work together for my good. I praise You for Your great love and mercy.

El-Channun ... The Gracious God

Oh that My people would listen to Me ... Psalm 81:13

Prayer Response to Psalm 81

You, oh Lord, are worthy of all honor, worship, and praise. How joyful it is when Your children gather and sing songs of praise and worship You with instruments. You are glorified when Your children assemble and testify of Your greatness. But not only do we need to praise You, we need to hear from You.

As Israel assembled, You spoke to the people and reminded them of their bondage in Egypt and how You freed them. You reminded them to reflect on the many ways You provided for them and the miracles of grace You performed on their behalf. Help me, Father, to listen as You speak to me from Your Word and help me to remember all that You have done in my life.

You reminded the children of Israel of the times they called on You in their troubles and how You answered their prayers. Oh Father, You have done the same for me and I thank You. But Lord, You also require obedience. The nation of Israel failed to obey the first command and so You admonished them.

Your Word makes it plain that You are a jealous God and we are to have no other gods but You. It is evident that You do not tolerate pretense. You see right through it and judge accordingly. I pray that I will not allow any other person or thing to take precedence over You, Lord. My heart's desire is to walk humbly with You and to listen and obey You. Protect my heart from stubbornness and hypocrisy, and enable me to heed Your Word. As Your child, I pray that I will not disappoint You, and I will continue to walk with You and be satisfied. I praise and thank You for Your faithfulness.

El Hanne'eman ... The Faithful God

Arise, O God, judge the earth! For it is You who possesses all the nations. Psalm 82:8

Prayer Response to Psalm 82

Sovereign and righteous Lord, in the midst of this world with all its unrighteous leaders, You are still on the throne. You are still God Almighty, the King of Kings and Lord of Lords. You are the only One Who sees and knows all things and are able to rule with perfect justice. As evidenced by the chaos in our world, our leaders do not lead with justice and most of them seem to rule with evil intent. This was true in Israel and is still true today. Your warning to our national leaders is to care about the people, especially the most vulnerable in society.

Father, I pray that our national leaders would heed that warning and show concern about the needs of the people, instead of promoting their own egos and agendas. Give them kind and tender hearts so they will care about the weak and those who are fatherless. Many of our leaders are so self-absorbed that they give no regard to those who are afflicted and destitute. In fact, they look with disdain upon those who are less fortunate. God, forgive our leaders, humble them, and cause them to see that You are the source of life itself.

Help them understand that all people are created in Your image and all people have worth. You have created every person with a purpose and plan, and we are all dependent upon You, whether we acknowledge it or not. No one can breathe a breath without Your grace. Without You, leaders would not have the ability to lead. Forgive our leaders for their arrogance and greed. Cleanse their hearts and fill them with Your love.

There is coming a day when Jesus will return and will reign with perfect righteousness, but until then I pray for our leaders. Remind them that their leadership is temporary and they are mortal. They need Jesus. Remind them that when they die, they must stand before You and give an account to You. Have mercy on the leaders of the world and each nation they represent.

El Elyon ... The Most High God

That they may know that You alone, whose name is the Lord,
are the Most High over all the earth. Psalm 83:18

Prayer Response to Psalm 83

You, oh God, are omniscient and omnipresent. There is never a moment in time when You are not aware of what is going on in this world. You are at work even when we do not see it.

In this Psalm, Israel's enemies are plotting against them and Asaph calls on You to intervene. These nations were heathen nations with great power. But Asaph knew they were no match for You, and he appeals for Your help. Just as You created the earth with a word, You could defeat them with the power of Your Word. After all, You miraculously defeated Israel's enemies many times.

Today, evil nations still conspire against Israel, and I pray that You will continue to watch over, protect, and preserve that nation. I also pray for Your divine intervention in the affairs of the United States since we, too, have many nations which wish to destroy us. Protect Your purposes and plans for our nation and Israel.

Evil against Your children, the church, is also more and more pronounced all around the world. The enemy of our souls is enraged and persecution is heightened. Even in this country, we are beginning to see freedoms taken away and people becoming less tolerant of Christianity. Much of the prophesies from Your Word are unfolding before our eyes.

Because You are sovereign, I ask that You intervene and act in accordance with Your perfect plan and will. Jesus warned us that as we approach the end time, evil would increase and persecution would come. I pray that each of Your children will stand strong in the finished work of Christ and that we be found faithful when Jesus returns.

Physical and spiritual enemies are out to destroy Your Word and Your children. But You are greater! You miraculously won many victories for Israel and You are still a God of miracles today. You are the same yesterday, today, and forever. I am thankful that in Christ the final victory has already been won for those who know Jesus. Your

Word tells us how the story ends. Keep me focused on Jesus and not on events and circumstances. You are indeed the Most High God, over all the earth. There is no need to fear or be dismayed.

El Elyon ... The Most High God

For the Lord God is a sun and shield; the Lord gives grace and glory; no good thing does He withhold from those who walk uprightly. Psalm 84:11

Prayer Response to Psalm 84

Everlasting Father, how blessed I am that Your presence abides within me and I do not need to go to a particular place to worship You. I can lift my heart in praise and worship to You at any time and place.

As I read this Psalm, I can sense the longing in the heart of the psalmist to be in Your holy temple, because there he would be in Your presence. The psalmist is even envious of the birds who get to nest there and be close to You.

Oh Father, Your presence is what I long for. Just as the birds found protection under the eaves of the temple, so I am protected in You. I do love to enter Your house of worship and miss it when I am unable to be there. Fellowship with You and others is a joy and delight. Help me and all Your children determine to prepare our hearts before we enter Your house and to anticipate a time of worship. In this Psalm, many of the worshipers had to travel through difficult places and they needed Your strength. But they remained determined and steadfast because it was important. Many of Your children face rough and fearful situations, but in Your presence there is blessing. Just as You sent autumn rains to quench the dry earth, so You provide blessings and relief for Your children.

You satisfy my needs and bring refreshment. Your Word reminds me that adversity produces endurance and maturity, and in my weakness You are strong. Help me draw near to You because You promise to draw near to me. You provide everything I need for my spiritual journey.

Prayer is a big part of worship and I thank You for listening and answering my prayers. Because I come in Jesus' name, I can pray with confidence, knowing that I will receive Your grace when I need it. The psalmist desired Your presence so much that he would settle for being a doorkeeper in Your house, over fame, power, and wealth. Father, I pray that I maintain that humble attitude.

Remind me often that You are the source of light, truth, and joy. It is You Who protects and grants favor and honor. You are a gracious Father and You withhold no good thing from Your children. I can be at peace because my confidence is in You. I am blessed that through Christ I have a right relationship with You, and I pray that You will keep me close and free from sin. How blessed I am. You are the Lord of Hosts.

El Hashamayim ... The God of the Heavens

Will You not Yourself revive us again, that Your people may rejoice in You? Show us Your lovingkindness, O Lord, and grant us Your salvation. Psalm 85:6–7

Prayer Response to Psalm 85

Gracious and merciful God, this Psalm reminds me to be thankful for Your favor and restoration. I am thankful that even when I have turned away, You have not forsaken me, but instead pursued and restored me.

Over and over, You showed Your mercy and forgiveness to a rebellious Israel. When they confessed their sin and repented, You forgave and restored them. Help me to remember Your mercies from the past and to remember that, even in discipline, Your goal is always restoration. You desire fellowship with Your children.

I pray that, as a nation, we would remember our beginnings. Help us remember the godly principles upon which our nation was founded. We have sinned greatly, and You have every right to be angry; we certainly deserve Your wrath. Our sin is oppressing our country, and I ask that in Your mercy You would deliver us from our sin. Bring us to our knees so that we will confess our sin and repent.

I praise and thank You for Jesus, Who sacrificed His life and satisfied Your righteous requirement for forgiveness. In Christ, my sins are forgiven, they are covered, and I stand before You, righteous in Jesus. There is no condemnation in Him. Grant me Your boldness to share that Good News with others.

Just as the psalmist cries out for restoration and revival, I, too, pray for restoration and revival for the United States. I pray that You would pour out Your Spirit and send revival to Your children. Many of us are on life support and we desperately need our spiritual lives revived and renewed. Our country was once a great nation, but that was because of Your grace and favor as we acknowledged and depended upon You. We have lost our way and only You can bring us back.

I pray for revival for myself and my loved ones, for my pastor and congregation, and all the churches in my community. I know that

I cannot work up revival; only You can send it. Have mercy on our nation, just as You did for Nineveh—not because we deserve it, but because You are merciful and good.

I pray that, even in these difficult days, You will speak peace to those who know and love You. Keep us humble before You. And when You do show us mercy and forgive our sins, keep us from turning again. You are mercy, truth, righteousness, and peace. I praise You for Who You are and that I am forever Yours.

El Malei Rachamim ... All Merciful God

Teach me Your way, O Lord; I will walk in Your truth; unite my heart to fear Your name. Psalm 86:11

Prayer Response to Psalm 86

Gracious and forgiving Lord, please keep me humble like David. Enable me to recognize my inadequacies and my needs, always acknowledging Your grace and forgiveness through Jesus. Thank You for Your goodness and loving-kindness. I am dependent upon You for life itself and it is You Who preserves my soul.

Thank You for always hearing my prayers and supplications, especially in times of trouble and heartache. Thank You for answering them even when I do not see the answer or it is delayed.

There is no one in heaven or earth that can compare to You. You are God Almighty, and I pray that You will continue to reveal to me more and more of Yourself. Continue to teach me Your truths and enable me to apply them in my life and walk in Your ways. I praise You for Who You are and all the wonderful things You have done in my life and continue to do. I look forward to the day when everyone will acknowledge and worship You.

It is so easy to sometimes get sidetracked by so many worldly concerns. Please guard my heart and help me focus on Jesus, the author and finisher of my faith. Protect me from a divided heart. Give me a thankful heart, a heart that fears You and glorifies Your name. You are indeed merciful, gracious, loving, kind, patient, and truthful. I praise You for Your grace to face the challenges each day brings and the strength that You alone provide. Thank You for Your mercies that are new each morning. I cannot even begin to count the times You have come to my rescue and comforted my soul. Thank You for being my loving Heavenly Father and for the fact that You are always with me.

El Hannora ... The Awesome God

All my springs of joy are in You. Psalm 87:7

Prayer Response to Psalm 87

God of Israel and the nations of the world, I am not sure that I fully understand this Psalm, but I do know that You chose the nation of Israel to be a light to the rest of the world. They failed to be that light, and You eventually sent Your Son Jesus to be that Light. You made a covenant with Israel and over and over Your Word tells us that You love Israel with an everlasting love.

Jerusalem was Your choice for the location of the temple where people came to worship You and enjoy Your presence. The beautiful mountains that You created and positioned around that city are not holy within themselves, but are holy because of Your presence. Many of the men in Scripture had encounters with You on those mountains.

I thank You that I encounter You every day. My body is now the temple, and I can commune with You any time and any place. Thank You, Jesus, for making this possible. You have told me to be holy because You are holy. Within myself I know that my righteousness is as filthy rags, but, thankfully, I can stand before You in the righteousness of Christ Jesus. His presence in me makes me holy in Your sight.

One day, Jesus will return and will rule and reign in new Jerusalem with perfect righteousness. Peace will finally reign. Your Word reveals that every nation and tongue will be represented among the redeemed. From the beginning of time, Your plan and purposes are being fulfilled. You know who will and will not be counted in the number of those who accept Jesus as Savior and Lord. You alone, Father, know when all things will be fulfilled.

Jesus is the Rock, the foundation upon which the church is established. In Your time, all the nations will gather in Zion and will worship You. Like the psalmist, I recognize that You are the source of my life, joy, and happiness. All my springs of joy are in You!

El Yisrael ... God of Israel

O Lord, the God of my salvation, I have cried out by day and in the night before You. Psalm 88:1

Prayer Response to Psalm 88

Loving and merciful Father, as Your child I am not exempt from trouble. Even Paul acknowledged it is through many tribulations that we enter Your kingdom. Like the psalmist, there have been times, Lord, when I did not understand why You seemed to be silent when I called out to You for help. There have been times when the burdens of life seemed more than I could bear. Yet things got worse instead of better. I have experienced times when my strength was gone and I had no desire to go forward. But, Father, in those times I had no place to turn but to You. And even though I could not readily see or hear You, Your presence remained.

You have promised to never leave nor forsake me. Your Word encouraged, comforted, and strengthened me. You reminded me of Your great love toward me and that You are always faithful. Your Word reminded me that You cause all things to work together for my good, including the not so good. You reminded me of all the suffering Jesus went through on my behalf. My suffering does not even begin to compare! You reminded me that the suffering in this life is temporary and that I have the joy of eternity with Jesus to look forward to. I thank You for Your patience and grace to keep keeping on.

In the midst of life's heartaches and struggles, I thank You for Your strength and Your joy. I thank You for Your presence and abiding love, and I praise You that I belong to You and my life is secure in Your hands. Help me to trust You with all my heart and not try to figure out the whys.

El Roi ... The God Who Sees Me

O Lord God of hosts, who is like You, O mighty Lord? Your faithfulness also surrounds You. Psalm 89:8

Prayer Response to Psalm 89

Loving and faithful Father, I want to be like Ethan, sharing Your great love, mercy, and faithfulness to the next generation.

You inhabit the praises of Your people, so help me praise You in every circumstance because You do not change. Your character is forever the same. You are faithful to fulfill all Your promises. Your faithfulness and greatness are visually seen throughout the heavens and the earth. There is no one mighty like You and no one can be compared to You. You alone are God Almighty and deserve my reverence and praise.

In Christ, all things were created and for His good pleasure. It all belongs to You and You hold it all together. Not only are You mighty in power and strength, but You are good. You are righteous and just, merciful and true.

How blessed I am to be Your child. Thank You for sending Jesus to make this possible. Through Jesus Christ I am an adopted child, a child of the King! In Jesus I have joy, and He has imparted to me His righteousness. He lights my way and strengthens me. In Christ I experience Your favor and You are my Rock and shield.

Lord, I want to be like David, whose heart belonged to You. You chose him to be king of Israel. You anointed, established, strengthened, and exalted David. But David was mortal and his kingdom ended. However, through his bloodline would come the Messiah, Jesus. His kingdom will last forever.

Israel failed to keep the covenant that You made with them. But despite their unfaithfulness, You have remained faithful. And despite my unfaithfulness, You are always faithful to me. As Israel sinned and judgment came, You always forgave and restored them when they confessed and turned back to You. Thank You for the forgiveness I have in Christ. If I confess my sin, You are faithful and just and You forgive and cleanse. I praise You that Your mercies are new every morning. I give You praise and thanks!

EL Hanne'eman ... The Faithful God

So teach us to number our days, that we may present to You a heart of wisdom. Psalm 90:12

Prayer Response to Psalm 90

You, oh Lord, are the Alpha and Omega, the beginning and the end. My mind cannot grasp that You existed before there was anything and that time has no relevance for You. For me, the years are flying by, but to You a thousand years is like a day! Eternity is impossible to comprehend.

You created everything I see and cannot see, and sustain it all. You know all things and see all things, even the sins that I think are secret. But despite my sin and frailties, You love me and are merciful and kind.

This Psalm reminds me that my life on earth is full of work and sorrow, and it is also short. Moses understood the brevity of life. Please, Lord, continue to teach me this truth and give me grace to redeem the time that I have remaining. Give me a heart of wisdom and guide my steps so I do not waste Your precious gift of time. Life is so uncertain, and You have created me and redeemed me for Your divine purposes. I want to be faithful in fulfilling Your purpose for my life.

Oh Father, keep me close to You. It is only in You that I find peace, joy, strength, forgiveness, and satisfaction. I praise You for Your compassion, mercy, and blessing. Without Your blessing, whatever I do will have little impact. Without Jesus, I can do nothing. Continue to grace me with Your favor. I love You, Lord.

EL Olam ... The Everlasting God

He who dwells in the shelter of the Most High will abide in the shadow of the Almighty. Psalm 91:1

Prayer Response to Psalm 91

Loving Father, this Psalm encourages and comforts my heart every time I read it. Living with You gives me such peace. Thank You for Your abiding presence and, oh, how I long to remain sheltered in You!

Forgive me when I stray, and may Your Holy Spirit continually convict and draw me back to that secret place. My life has been good and You have blessed me in so many ways. It would be impossible to recall all Your blessings.

But life in this sinful world dishes out many troubles, as well. Jesus told us that in this life there will be much tribulation. It is during those times when I am so thankful that I can take shelter in You. When the circumstances of life are overwhelming, You are my refuge and fortress. Like the mother bird who protects her baby chicks, I am protected under Your wings. You are my shield in the spiritual battles that I face. When Satan hurls his fiery darts, You dispatch Your angels to watch over me. I have no idea how many times they have preserved my life and protected my way.

In Your great love, You have given me salvation through faith in Your Son Jesus Christ. Thank You for the forgiveness of sin and eternal life. It is because You first loved me that I can love You. You hear and answer my prayers and You have promised to never leave me. You are with me in my troubles, and in Christ I am victorious because He has already won the battle.

You shower Your blessings upon me and give me a satisfying life. When I breathe my last breath on earth, I will see Jesus face-to-face and my salvation will be complete. You are my faithful Heavenly Father, and I praise and thank You that I belong to You.

El Yeshuati ... The God of My Salvation

The righteous man will flourish like the palm tree ... They will still yield fruit in old age; they shall be full of sap and very green. Psalm 92:12, 14

Prayer Response to Psalm 92

Gracious and loving Father, You have blessed me in so many ways, and I am so thankful to be Your child. Each morning when I awake, I realize You have graced me with another day and that You have a plan and a purpose for me.

Each night that I lay my head down for bed, I praise You for Your faithfulness in guiding me through another day. It is easy to sing praises to You because of Who You are and all Your awesome works.

There are so many things I do not understand. Because You are Almighty God, Your thoughts and ways are so much higher than mine. But I am thankful for the knowledge You have given to me through Your Word. You reveal to me the things I need to know.

I pray for those who ignore or reject Your Word. They may or may not have worldly success, but they are unprepared for eternity. Open their eyes and draw them to Jesus. I especially pray for my loved ones and ask that You save them before it is too late. I praise and thank You for Your strength and for refreshing me with Your Word. I acknowledge that the only righteousness I have is in Jesus.

Thank You for encouraging me that in Christ I am strong like the cedar and fruitful like the palm. I claim Your promise that even in old age my life will yield forth the fruit of righteousness. Please, Lord, keep my life fresh and renewed and Your Holy Spirit freely flowing in and through me. May I continue to abide in You. You, oh Lord, are holy and righteous, and You are my solid foundation, my Rock!

El Gibbor ... The Mighty God

Your throne is established from of old; You are from everlasting.
Psalm 93:2

Prayer Response to Psalm 93

Everlasting and sovereign Lord, You are from everlasting to everlasting and more majestic than my mind can possibly comprehend. Your strength, power, and might are unimaginable. You are much greater than any of the powers on earth, much mightier than the roaring and crashing waves of many waters. There is nothing and no one I can compare You with and nothing can frustrate Your plans or change Your promises.

Your Word is eternal. You created the world out of nothing and sustain it all. It will remain until You say so. You are my holy and awesome God, and You rule and reign with power and might.

El Hannora ... The Awesome God

Prayer Response to Psalm 94

Righteous Judge, this Psalm could easily be written today because wickedness abounds. Lying, murder, destruction, arrogance, and outright persecution of Your children are everywhere. Since there is no fear or acknowledgement of You, people continue in their sinful ways, with no concern of the consequences or eternal judgment.

Father, I acknowledge that You are sovereign, righteous, and just. Not only do You see and hear all things, but You even know the thoughts and intentions of every person. Help me not to dwell on all the wickedness and injustices of this world because that only leads to discouragement. Keep my focus on Your Word, on Jesus, and Your promise that You will never leave me and that righteousness will prevail. You promised if my mind is stayed on You, in peace You will keep me. Help me to rest in You.

You drew me unto salvation and it is You Who keeps my soul. I praise You for Your mercy and grace. When anxieties try to take over my mind, Holy Spirit, remind me of Your Word and comfort my heart. Lord, staying in fellowship with You is vital, so please keep me in Your Word, and if I get off track, do the necessary things to set my course straight. You discipline those You love. I entrust myself to You, and I must leave the judgment of others in Your hands, as well.

Jesus, You are my defender, Rock, and refuge, and I am secure in You. You are holy, righteous, and just, and also gracious, merciful, and patient. It is not Your desire that any should perish. I pray for those who continue in their evil ways, because unless they repent and turn to Jesus, they will face eternal judgment in hell. Open their eyes and enlighten their hearts; draw them to Jesus before it is too late.

Jesus, You are coming back and this time You are coming to judge the unrighteous. You will rule and reign, and justice and righteousness will prevail. You are the King of Kings and Lord of Lords! Hallelujah!

El Tsaddik ... The Righteous God

Let us come before His presence with thanksgiving, let us shout joyfully to Him with psalms. Psalm 95:2

Prayer Response to Psalm 95

Great and mighty God, You are worthy of all praise and thanksgiving because every good and perfect gift comes from You. I praise You with singing and I praise You with a joyful and enthusiastic heart. I especially praise and thank You for Jesus and the gift of salvation I have received by faith in Him. He is my Rock and in Him I am secure. I praise You for Your presence and ask that I gain a greater awareness of Your presence each moment of the day.

I pray You will remind me often of Your greatness so that I may honor and worship You. You alone are God and Creator of heaven and earth. From the lowest valleys to the highest mountains, and from the seas to dry land, You created it all. It all belongs to You, including man, who is formed in Your image. Your power and majesty are clearly seen in all of Your creation.

You are my great and mighty Shepherd, and I am humbled to be Your sheep. Thank You for calling me unto salvation and giving me the faith to believe and receive Jesus. Your call for salvation goes out to everyone who will call upon the name of Your Son. I pray for those who continue to harden their hearts against You and refuse to believe and trust You. The children of Israel who hardened their hearts in disbelief did not enter the Promised Land and those who do not trust You today will not enter Your rest nor spend eternity with You. Open their eyes that they will see Your greatness and eternal love. Draw them to Jesus.

El Haggadol ... The Great God

Sing to the Lord, bless His name; proclaim good tidings of His salvation from day to day. Tell of His glory among the nations, His wonderful deeds among all the peoples. For great is the Lord and greatly to be praised; He is to be feared above all gods. Psalm 96:2–4

Prayer Response to Psalm 96

Lord of heaven and earth, Your mercies and grace are new every day, giving me another day and another reason to praise You. I praise You for Your gift of salvation in Christ and ask that You give me the boldness I need to tell others that Jesus saves.

You are so great and mighty, and the whole world needs to know that You alone are God and worthy of honor and praise. All other so-called gods are man-made idols. Enable the peoples of the earth to see Your majesty, strength, and glory so that they will bow down and worship You. You created the heavens and the earth out of nothing but Your spoken word. It is firmly established and will not be moved unless You say so.

You alone are sovereign Lord. You are righteous and holy and, one day, Your Son Jesus is returning to judge all peoples. May Your children be found faithful. You, oh Lord, are faithful and just, and will judge the world with perfect righteousness.

El Tsaddik ... The Righteous God

Prayer Response to Psalm 97

Jehovah God, You are our infinite, eternal Maker, and with mighty power You reign as ruler over this world. Lord, You are so holy that no man could ever look upon You and live. You are all-powerful and absolutely righteous and just in every way.

Like You did for the children of Israel at Mount Sinai, teach us to fear You. You are mightier than the mountains and absolutely nothing can thwart Your plans. Every person on earth has witnessed Your glory in the heavens and on the earth and are without excuse to not worship You. Those who worship anyone or anything other than You should be ashamed because You alone are God.

Everyone on earth benefits from Your goodness, but as Your child I rejoice in Your divine revelation. You have loved me with an everlasting love so that I can in turn love You. Help me to love the things that You love and to hate the evil that You hate.

You sent Your Son Jesus to die on a cross to save my soul, and it is Jesus Who preserves me. He has delivered me from a sinful and worldly life and the Light has shown the Way. I rejoice in His salvation and the righteousness that He imparts. Praise the name of Jesus! One day, every knee will bow and every tongue confess that He is Lord.

El Olam ... The Everlasting God

The Lord has made known His salvation; He has revealed His righteousness in the sight of the nations. Psalm 98:2

Prayer Response to Psalm 98

Lord and Savior, I can always praise You for my salvation and it never grows old. Each new day brings new opportunities to praise You because You are always at work in my life and in the lives of others. Each day You are doing wonderful things. Open my eyes to see You in every situation.

I praise You for Your divine revelation in all creation, for all the world to see. Your strength and power are evident to all. From Genesis to Revelation, Your Word testifies that You have consistently revealed to man Your love, salvation, and righteousness. At the appointed time You sent Your Son Jesus as Your ultimate revelation. Jesus said that those who saw Him, saw the Father. Jesus was and is the Savior of the world. Even though Your chosen nation at large rejected Him, Your loving-kindness and faithfulness to Israel remain. The people of Israel broke their covenant with You, but You always remain faithful because that is Who You are.

The Good News of the Gospel is being spread throughout the world, to all the nations, so that peoples from every tongue can rejoice in Your salvation. Even the mountains and the seas give praise to the King of Kings and Lord of Lords! If nature can praise You, surely Your children can praise You with joyful shouts, singing, and the sounds of many instruments.

We can praise You because Jesus is coming to earth again. He came the first time to be our sacrificial Lamb, but this time He will come as righteous Judge. He will rightfully rule and reign in perfect righteousness and will judge the world with perfect equity. Even so, come!

El Hanne'eman ... The Faithful God

Exalt the Lord our God and worship at His holy hill, for the
Lord our God is holy. Psalm 99:9

Prayer Response to Psalm 99

K ing of Kings and Lord of Lords, it gives me great comfort to know that You rule and reign over the earth. You are all-seeing, all-knowing, ever present, all-powerful, and completely sovereign. You are great and awesome, deserving honor, and worthy of all praise. You are loving, merciful, gracious, kind, and forgiving, and You are holy.

Your holiness is beyond my understanding because I have never witnessed pure holiness. Your holiness reminds me that I am sinful and unrighteous and that I need Jesus. You have established a perfect standard, and I can only come before You in His righteousness.

The priests and prophets of old trusted and obeyed Your commands. They called on Your name as they looked to You for wisdom, understanding, direction, and protection, and You answered them. Those patriarchs set an example for Your children to follow. Help me to seek You in all things. Those great men of faith were not perfect. They sinned, just like me. But You revealed to them that You are forgiving. Thank You for forgiving my sin when I confess and repent.

But even when I do not repent, You are loving, and discipline me so that I will return to You for forgiveness and restoration. Thank You for such great love and for never letting go of me. You are faithful and I am forever Yours. I praise, honor, and worship You!

El Elyon ... The Most High God

I will sing of lovingkindness and justice; to You, O Lord, I will sing praises. Psalm 101:1

Prayer Response to Psalm 100

Creator of heaven and earth and God of the nations, every nation on earth should recognize Your majesty through creation and providential care. People are without excuse to know that You are God Almighty.

Because of Who You are, it is a privilege and duty to serve You joyfully and sing praises unto You. I praise You because I am convinced that You are my God and Creator. You have called me and redeemed me. I am Your child, and You are my Shepherd and keeper. You are my loving Father Who cares for me.

I thank You and praise You for Your goodness, mercy, everlasting truth, and Your faithfulness to all generations. One day, every knee will bow and every tongue will confess that You are Lord.

El Echad ... The One God

Prayer Response to Psalm 101

Merciful and loving Father, I praise You for Your mercy and justice. I ask that You instill within me a balance of both. As King, David knew that his obedience to You was essential if he wanted Your blessing. I, too, desire to live wisely and pleasing to You so that I can maintain a close and right relationship with You.

I am confident that You never leave me, but I do not want anything to get in the way of our fellowship. I pray that my walk with You will be consistent, whether I am at home or in public. Keep my heart and mind stayed upon You. Guard my heart and mind and deliver me from wickedness. I do not want to be among those who fall away. Keep my feet on the straight and narrow path.

David opposed those who slandered others and those who were prideful and arrogant. He also rejected those who were deceitful and liars. Your Word tells me these character traits are an abomination to You. Please, Father, keep me humble, guard my attitudes and words, and help me to always speak the truth in love.

Father, it is my desire to remain faithful to You, stay close to You, and serve You for the time that I have remaining. Thank You for the promise that You began the good work in me and You will complete it. I rest in that promise. Praise the Lord!

El Malei Rachamim ... All Merciful God

This will be written for the generation to come, that a people yet to be created may praise the Lord. Psalm 102:18

Prayer Response to Psalm 102

God of all comfort, in times of crisis I especially need the reassurance of Your presence. I thank You for the promise that You will never leave me. In those times, I call out to You and I look for a speedy answer.

There have been times, Lord, when I felt like the psalmist: weak, exhausted, lonely. Yet I claim Your promise; You are with me. My spiritual enemy uses the difficulties of life to try and discourage me and get me to doubt Your love for me. But Your Word reminds me that You love me with an everlasting love. My enemy tries to trick me into believing that, for some reason, You have rejected me. But Your Word reminds me that nothing can snatch me out of Your hand and even in discipline You love me.

Focusing on the crisis brings me down, but keeping my focus on You and Your Word lifts me out of discouragement and despair. Even in those times, like the psalmist, I need to look outward. Not only do I need Your mercy, but so many people around me need Your mercy and grace. I need to be that vessel through which they can see You.

The psalmist was encouraged by focusing on Your favor to Jerusalem and the fact that one day You will be exalted among all the nations. I, too, can be encouraged by looking back at Your past blessings and looking forward to the glorious hope I have in Christ. Your love letter to us has also recorded Your loving-kindness to Your chosen ones. There is testimony upon testimony throughout Scripture of Your love, mercy, and grace, so that future generations will know of Your greatness.

Even in this text, I am reminded that You see all things, hear our cries, redeem us, gather us together to serve You, and You accept our service. Because You have created us, You are aware of our weaknesses. Your Word reminds me that in my weakness, You are strong. You are from everlasting to everlasting and You never change.

I, on the other hand, am mortal, and life on earth is constantly changing. I am thankful that You are the one constant in my life; I can always trust and depend on You.

I praise and thank You for Your great salvation and for allowing me to be Your child. Help me be faithful to You and in sharing Your great love to the next generation.

El Roi ... The God Who Sees Me

The Lord is compassionate and gracious, slow to anger and abounding in lovingkindness. Psalm 103:8

Prayer Response to Psalm 103

Sovereign and awesome God, this Psalm reminds me of some of the reasons why I need to bless and praise You with my body, soul, and spirit. First and foremost, by Your grace You have forgiven my sins and iniquities. In Your perfect love, You sent Jesus to shed His blood on a cross, to be the propitiation for my sin. I can now stand before You in the name of Jesus, as if I had never sinned. Jesus' blood has washed me whiter than snow and I can now have fellowship with You.

Lord, You are also my Great Physician. It is You Who heals my body when it becomes sick and weak; You restore me. When I am spiritually weak, it is You Who restores my soul and renews my spirit. Only in You do I find strength that endures.

You have redeemed my life from a path of unrighteousness and have protected and preserved my life. I have been the recipient of Your loving-kindness and compassion, and it is You Who satisfies my life. Every good and perfect gift comes from You.

Father, You are merciful, gracious, and patient with me, and I praise You that You do not execute the judgment I deserve. But even Your judgments are tempered with grace. You are a holy and righteous God, and apart from Jesus my righteousness is like filthy rags. I deserve Your judgment. Because of Your great love, You have chosen to not only forgive but to remove my transgressions as far as the east is to the west.

Your compassion is immeasurable and You gladly pour it out to me and all Your children. Because You created us, You know that our frame is weak and our time on earth is limited, just like every other created thing. You are from everlasting to everlasting and You do not change. Your compassion will continue from generation to generation to those who love, trust, and obey You. You are Lord of heaven and earth.

The angels are Your messengers and heavenly hosts who listen to You and obey Your assignments. How they must praise You for the strength You give them and the privilege to serve Almighty God.

All of creation points to You, Creator of heaven and earth. The mountains, oceans, heavens, and every created thing praises You. How can I not bless and praise You, Almighty God, my Savior and Lord!

El Hannora ... The Awesome God

O Lord, how many are Your works! In wisdom You have made them all; the earth is full of Your possessions. Psalm 104:24

Prayer Response to Psalm 104

Great and mighty God, Your majesty and power are evident everywhere, and I give You honor and praise. You are holy and righteous, and if it were not for Jesus I would be unable to approach You. Your power is clearly seen in all of creation, in the waters, clouds, and wind. And though I cannot see angels, You rule over them, commissioning and equipping them to do Your will.

All things were created by You and firmly established. The foundations cannot be moved unless You move them. The mountains stand and, amazingly, You established boundaries for the oceans and rivers, and they cannot go beyond those boundaries! It is You Who provides water to the wild animals, and the birds praise You with song for Your providential care. You cause the grass to grow for cattle and provide vegetation for mankind. You provide grapes for wine and grain to make bread. I praise You that You provide for all our basic needs and for the needs of all Your creatures.

The sun and the moon were firmly established by You and each day and night they faithfully rise and set. Everything operates according to Your plan. The animals depend upon Your provisions at night. Men and women labor for food during the day, yet still are dependent upon You for the harvest. Your wisdom and perfect order are visible everywhere: in the heavens, on earth, and in the sea. All of creation is dependent upon You for provision and for life and breath itself. Without You, we would perish.

I praise You for the outpouring of Your Spirit—Your presence and favor upon Your creation. I am confident You delight in all that You have created, and I want my life to bring You honor. I pray that in my remaining years You will enable me to focus on Your greatness and goodness. Help me to praise You with songs and meditations of Your Word in my heart and mind.

Remind me often that the wicked things of this world are passing away and that Jesus has overcome the world. Man is sinful by nature, but Jesus is Your provision for salvation. He is the Way, the Truth, and the Life, and there is salvation in no other. Thank You for saving me, and give me boldness to share with others the hope I have in Jesus. I praise You that You are Lord of my life.

El Gibbor ... The Mighty God

Seek the Lord and His strength; seek His face continually.
Psalm 105:4

Prayer Response to Psalm 105

Gracious Heavenly Father, I am reminded once again to thank You for all the wonderful blessings of life. I am also reminded that I must tell others about the wonderful things You do and how awesome You are. Not only must I seek You and praise You, but I must point others to You so they will know You and call upon Your name.

This Psalm is a call for Israel to remember the past and the multitude of ways You cared for them as a nation. The psalmist remembered how You protected the prophets and the patriarchs of old and how You used Joseph to preserve the nation during a time of famine. You also allowed Israel to grow in number and strength and You sent Your servant Moses to deliver them from bondage in Egypt. All the peoples witnessed Your miraculous power as judgment after judgment came upon Egypt. You delivered Your children with resources of gold and silver. And while Israel was in the wilderness, You gave them light at night and a cloud of protection during the day. You also supplied them with bread and meat to eat and water to drink. Despite their rebellious spirit and unbelief, You eventually brought Israel into the Promised Land.

Your providential care is so evident throughout Your Word, and is so evident throughout my life, as well. Just as You have always remained faithful to Israel, You have remained faithful to me, even when I am not. You have guided and directed my life, strengthened me, and allowed me to grow in Your grace. I recognize that is You Who has provided for my needs and protected me over the years. You have never left me and You keep all Your promises.

Like Israel, I, too, am sometimes disobedient, and yet Your forgiveness and restoration are readily available. You led Israel through some difficult times on their way to the Promised Land. But just as You promised, they did enter it. You have promised me the gift of eternal life in heaven with Jesus because I have put my faith and trust in His saving grace. The journey has not always been smooth, but You have always seen me through. I am confident the work You began in me will be completed and one day I will enter the Promised Land and see Jesus face-to-face. Until then, help me be faithful to Your Word and help me give You the praise and honor You deserve.

El-Channun ... The Gracious God

Save us, O Lord our God, and gather us from among the nations, to give thanks to Your holy name and glory in Your praise. Psalm 106:47

Prayer Response to Psalm 106

Heavenly Father, by nature You are absolutely holy and my nature is sinful. That is why I praise You for Your mercy and patience toward me. Even the praises from my lips are inadequate. However, words are not nearly as important as action, and You desire obedience. Lord, help me do the things that please You and bring You honor.

Thank You for Your gracious gift of salvation through Christ. I praise You for the benefits of knowing Jesus and the inheritance I share in Him.

As a nation, Israel sinned greatly against You. And I must confess the United States has also sinned greatly. Like Israel, we have forgotten the godly principles upon which we were founded. We have forgotten Your goodness and mercy. We have turned away from You and have sinned wickedly.

Despite Israel's continued disobedience, You delivered them for Your name's sake. I am asking You to do the same for our nation. Yet despite Your deliverances, Your people forgot Your goodness and rebelled again and again. They did not seek Your counsel and tested You. Their hearts were filled with worldly desires. Sometimes You gave them what they asked for even when it was not the best for them. Lord, help me seek Your will and not mine. Help us, as a nation, to do the same.

The sin of envy and pride caused Israel to experience Your judgment of fire and earthquake. Forgive me and cleanse me of any pride and envy, and forgive our nation. Israel turned from You to worship idols and if it were not for Moses' intercession, they would have been destroyed. Please forgive me for those idols that may be lurking in my heart and the many idols all around our world. I deserve and our nation deserves Your judgment, and I plead for Your mercy.

The children of Israel did not trust You to give them the Promised Land. They complained and refused to believe You. As a result, they wandered in the wilderness and did not get to enjoy the land flowing with milk and honey. Father, I pray that I will trust You and will be obedient to You because You alone are all-seeing and knowing. You know what is best for my life and what is best for the nation. You know what it will take to get us back on track.

When Israel worshipped Baal, You sent a plague. Once again You relented when someone interceded on their behalf. Lord, I pray for our nation that You relent and not pour out the judgment we deserve. Even Moses—as righteous as he was—in anger, disobeyed You. As a result he also did not get to enter the Promised Land. Father, how grateful I am for the forgiveness that is available to me through Jesus, because I fail You in so many ways every single day.

Israel became so sinful, the people were shedding innocent blood and even sacrificing their children to idols. Unfortunately, the United States is not much different. Our streets have become violent, with no regard to life, and babies are being aborted every day. Like Israel, we have defiled ourselves. I ask for Your forgiveness and divine intervention.

There were times when You were so angry with Israel that You allowed other nations to take them into captivity. Lord, I confess that is my fear for the United States. I do not know what You have in store for us as a nation, but I do know You do not forsake Your own. Each time Israel cried out to You in their affliction, You were merciful. Although Israel was never faithful in keeping their covenant with You, You were always faithful.

Father, because of Your faithfulness and mercy, I have hope not just for myself but also for our nation. I praise You that You are from everlasting to everlasting and that You do not change. You are the God of Israel and God of all nations, and my God and Heavenly Father.

El Malei Rachamim ... All Merciful God

Let the redeemed of the Lord say so, whom He has redeemed from the hand of the adversary ... Psalm 107:2

Prayer Response to Psalm 107

Good and merciful Lord, those two attributes are repeated throughout Scripture to describe You, and by experience I know this to be true. As Your child, I have every reason to declare to others Who You are. I pray that my words and my life will bear witness of Your grace.

You are my deliverer and provider. Just as You delivered Israel on many occasions from their enemies, You have delivered me from the enemy of my soul. And just as You provided Israel with their needs, You provide for mine. When Israel needed to be humbled, You humbled them, and You also do the same for me and all Your children. Because You love us so much, whatever situation we find ourselves in, we can call out to You for help and You will answer. You are the only One Who can satisfy the deep needs of our soul.

If only we could learn not to disobey You and rebel, we could avoid so much pain and heartache. But even in times of discipline from You, restoration is always the goal. Forgive me for the times that I am foolish and sin against You, and thank You for the forgiveness You freely give when I confess and repent. Whether I am physically ill or spiritually ill, You are the Great Physician.

When I face troubles that are self-inflicted or troubles due to life in a sinful world, You are my deliverer. Your power and goodness are evident through the transformations of the earth. You can make dry land into water springs and vice versa. It is You Who causes our crops and vineyards to grow and produce. It is You Who blesses mankind. It is You Who ministers to the oppressed, afflicted, and sorrowful, and You Who transforms their lives.

Open the eyes of those who do not seem to see Your goodness, and enlighten their hearts. Give them wisdom and understanding that they may know by experience Your great love for them. You loved the world so much that You sent Your Son Jesus to die on a cross, to redeem a lost and sinful world. Thank You for such a magnificent and wonderful gift.

El Hanne'eman ... The Faithful God

Be exalted, O God, above the heavens, and Your glory above all the earth. Psalm 108:5

Prayer Response to Psalm 108

My God and Father, like David, I recognize my strength and confidence is in You. Keep my heart clean, steadfast, and strong. All that I am and have are gifts from You and I praise You and give You thanks.

I pray that You will enable me to share Your love, mercy, and great salvation with others wherever I go. You are so awesome that the earth itself cannot contain Your glory. My praise is so inadequate, yet I praise You the best I can with my words and music.

Words are so inadequate to express my thankfulness for the salvation You have provided through Jesus. Your precious gift of salvation is offered freely to anyone who will believe and receive it. Open the eyes of the blinded, that they may see their need for salvation. Help all of us to grasp Your holiness so we can better understand our sinfulness and need for Jesus.

You, oh Lord, are the God of Israel, and You are also Lord of all the nations. Many nations do not acknowledge You, but that does not negate the truth that You are Lord. How much better off this world would be if every leader of every nation would depend upon You.

David fully understood that the only path to victory was dependence on You. Help me to always remember: Without Christ, I can do nothing. Without You, Lord, I am helpless. You are my help and my deliverer in times of need. My victories are found in You. How thankful I am that I belong to You.

El Hashamayim ... The God of the Heavens

With my mouth I will give thanks abundantly to the Lord;
and in the midst of many I will praise Him. Psalm 109:30

Prayer Response to Psalm 109

You, oh Lord, are righteous and just. It is evident that in this life, injustice abounds. And, like David, sometimes we are the object of injustice. People can be so deceitful, dishonest, and downright hateful without cause. Father, it is in these times that I struggle to maintain a right attitude and, more times than not, fail to look like Jesus. Please forgive me and give me the grace to grow in this area.

When David prayed, he looked to You for vengeance against his enemies. Jesus had not yet come, so David's prayer is different than mine. David did leave the judgment in Your hands, but Jesus says that I am to love my enemies and pray for those who despitefully use me. Apart from You, I am incapable of doing this.

Lord, I pray that You will pour out Your love in and through me in a miraculous way and enable me to faithfully pray for those who are hurtful. Help me, Father, not to react but to respond like Jesus. Sometimes it is those whom I deeply love that hurt me the most. But rather than pray for vengeance, I ask that You be merciful and convict them of their sin.

I realize how desperately I need You, because I am weak, poor, and needy. Remind me that those who say and do hurtful things are also weak, poor, and needy. I sometimes have difficulty separating the sin from the sinner. Just as You have delivered me from my sin and changed my life, You can do the same for them. We are all in need of Your mercy.

I praise You for all that You have done and continue to do in my life, and I pray that You will continue to work in the hearts and lives of those whom You have placed in my life. We are all broken and needy and desperately look to You for love, grace, and mercy. Thank You for Jesus and the gift of salvation I have in Him. I give You praise!

El Yeshuatenu ... The God of Our Salvation

The Lord says to my Lord: "Sit at My right hand until I make Your enemies a footstool for Your feet." Psalm 110:1

Prayer Response to Psalm 110

Everlasting God and Father, long before Jesus ever physically came to this earth in the form of man, He was with You, seated at Your right hand. He left all the glory of heaven in order to suffer and die for the sins of mankind. Jesus was the perfect sinless sacrifice so that man's relationship with You could be restored. The multitudes rejected Jesus, yet to everyone who believes in Him, You give the right to be called children of God.

Jesus, You are once again sitting at the right hand of the Father in heaven, and in the fulfillment of time You will rule and reign with perfect justice and peace. Until that day, the Gospel is being shared and spread abroad by those who believe and have received Your gift of salvation. It is You Who gives us the strength and power to tell others the Good News of the Gospel so that they, too, can be saved.

Lord, it gives me great comfort to know that You are my high priest and that You intercede daily on my behalf and on behalf of all who know You. You are compassionate, loving, and merciful, and You are holy. It is because You are holy that one day You will return to judge the nations and their rulers in righteousness. At that point it will be too late for those who have rejected Your gift of love. As Your child, I ask You to strengthen my will and empower me to share with people the Good News of the Gospel before it is too late. Thank You for saving my soul.

El Olam ... The Everlasting God

The fear of the Lord is the beginning of wisdom ... Psalm 111:10

Prayer Response to Psalm 111

Hallelujah! You are worthy of praise. I confess that I feel so inadequate in this area, and I pray I will be able to praise You without a divided heart. I admit that I have more difficulty with worship in public than I do in private because I am not able to fully focus on You with others around. Please enable me to praise You in church with the same fervor I praise You in private.

There is no question of Your greatness, honor, glory, and righteousness. Your greatness is seen not only in creation but in Your providential care. How important it is for me to remember Your goodness, grace, and mercy—to remember that it is You Who provides for my needs and keeps all Your promises.

Everything You do is done with fairness and justice. You are true to Your Word, which lasts forever. You are a holy God Who hates sin, but, in Your mercy, provided salvation for all peoples. Thank You for sending Your Son Jesus Who sacrificed His life for mine and imputed His righteousness to me. Now I can experience a right relationship with You and look forward to enjoying eternity in heaven.

I pray for those who do not recognize Your greatness and do not have a reverential fear of You, because that is where wisdom begins. According to Your Word, Christ is the wisdom of God. Open the eyes of people, that they will see their need for Jesus.

For me, Lord, I ask that I will continue to not only know You, but obey You. Jesus told us: "If you love Me, you will keep my commandments." (John 14:15) I do love You, but I am aware that I fail to meet up to Your standards daily. Thank You for the forgiveness Jesus provides. You are great and awesome, and I praise You for Who You are!

El Hakkavod ... The God of Glory

How blessed is the man who fears the Lord, who greatly delights in His commandments. Psalm 112:1

Prayer Response to Psalm 112

You alone, oh Lord, are worthy of praise! I thank You for instilling in my heart a reverent fear of You and a love for Your Word. Help me, Father, to be more obedient to You. Your Word promises blessings to those who fear You and obey You. I know that those blessings come in many forms and not necessarily in material blessings.

In Christ, I have been blessed with every spiritual blessing in heavenly places. But Your Word also assures me that You supply my every need. I know that is true and You have blessed me way beyond my needs.

I am fully aware that every good and perfect gift is from You, and I thank You and praise You for all that You have done and continue to do in my life. I especially thank You for Jesus and His righteousness, which has been imputed to me for eternity. Because I have placed my faith and trust in Christ's finished work, I am now Your child.

As Your child, I pray that Your light will shine forth from me, into this sinful dark world. Help me to deal with others graciously and to generously give. Guide me in all my decisions, that I will be a person of integrity. Enable me to stand strong and unwavering in the promises of Your Word. I pray that my trust in You will continue to grow until there is no doubt or fear and I pray that my life will cause others to desire to know You.

Help me, Lord, not to be overly concerned with those who will despise me because of You. Just as people rejected Your Son Jesus, I must come to grips with the fact that many will also reject me. Remind me each day that You are the only One I need to please and when I take my last breath, the only thing that will matter is my relationship with You. Thank You, Jesus, for dying for me and saving my soul!

El Channun ... The Gracious God

The Lord is high above all nations; His glory is above the heavens. Psalm 113:4

Prayer Response to Psalm 113

Lord of all the nations, the Psalms is a book of praise to You, my God, Lord, and Heavenly Father. Because I have been purchased by the precious blood of Jesus, I am honored to be Your servant and child. That alone is reason to praise Your name.

Each day when I wake up, I realize that You have given me this day as a gift and that You have things for me to accomplish. From morning to night, You are working in and through me, and reminding me of Your great love, grace, mercy, and forgiveness. I am humbled that despite Your immeasurable greatness, You care about me and everything and everyone You have created.

There is no one like You and the universe cannot contain You! Your glory exceeds my imagination. Yet despite Your majesty, You care about the poor and needy and the heartaches of those all around.

Lord, everyone is spiritually poor, needy, and barren. But You cared about our spiritual state and sent Your Son to redeem us. John 3:16 says it best: "For God so loved the world, that He gave His only begotten Son, that whoever believes in Him shall not perish, but have eternal life." I do not fully understand such love, but, oh, how thankful I am for it. Because of Jesus' sacrifice, I have been lifted out of darkness and into light. My sins are all forgiven and my life has purpose and meaning.

You are continually teaching me and molding me to be more like Jesus. And though I am not yet complete, one day I will get to see Him face-to-face and spend eternity with Him in heaven. Then, the good work that Jesus began in me will be complete! Praise Your name!

El Elyon ... The Most High God

Tremble, O earth, before the Lord ... Psalm 114:7

Prayer Response to Psalm 114

Father, this Psalm is about Your deliverance of Israel from Egypt. The Israelites were in bondage for over four hundred years. You heard the prayers of Your people and miraculously redeemed them and promised them a land flowing with milk and honey.

Because of Your redemption and Your promise fulfilled, Your children should forever be thankful and praise Your holy name. I, too, have been redeemed by You. I have been redeemed from the bondage of sin by the precious blood of Jesus, and You have promised an eternal home in heaven. While I await my eternal home, Your Word is filled with wonderful promises that are mine to enjoy now.

Thank You, Jesus, for making the ultimate sacrifice for me. Open the eyes of those who fail to see Your goodness and that You are a redeeming God. Pour out Your Spirit and draw men and women and boys and girls to Jesus. I especially pray for my loved ones who have not yet been redeemed. It is not Your will that anyone should perish. I praise and thank You in advance for answering my prayers.

El Haggadol ... The Great God

Prayer Response to Psalm 115

God of glory, You are continuously doing wonderful things in and through our lives, and we must learn to give You the praise You deserve. I pray that my works will point others to Jesus, and if I always give You the praise, no one should ever question Your presence.

Many people worship other things, like material possessions, power, and prestige. But You alone are our living sovereign God. Every other object of worship has been created, but You alone are our Creator. You are from everlasting to everlasting.

Just as Israel needed to trust You in all things, I do too. By Your grace, help me to trust You more. You are my help in times of trouble and my shield against the fiery darts of the enemy. Thank You for Your written Word which assures me of Your watchfulness and loving care. Thank You for the various ways that You bless my life. You are an impartial Father Who blesses all who fear You, and forgets no one. I continue to pray for my family and ask that You continue to work in each of our lives, drawing us in a closer walk with You. I would be lost without Your blessing of my life.

Lord, You created heaven and earth and it all belongs to You. Thank You for allowing us to enjoy all that You have created. While I am still alive and able, I want to praise You. I ask that in the few years remaining You will help me remain faithful and give You the honor and praise You deserve.

EL Hakkavod ... The God of Glory

Precious in the sight of the Lord is the death of His godly ones.
Psalm 116:15

Prayer Response to Psalms 116–117

Loving Father, these Psalms remind me that one reason I love You is because You are my Father and You listen to my prayers and answer them. I realize that is because You loved me long before I knew You. Because of Your love and answers to prayer, I continue to fellowship with You as You speak to me through Your Word.

Life has been filled with many troubles and difficulties, but I have looked to You for help, and You have guided me through them all. I praise You that You are gracious and merciful and that You have preserved my life. You are holy and righteous and, even though I am unholy and unrighteous, You loved me enough to save me by sending Your Son Jesus to die on a cross for my sin. Jesus did everything necessary to redeem me and imparted to me His righteousness. Thank You, Jesus, for such a wonderful gift!

Because of Your great love, there is no reason not to have peace in my soul. You have been good and faithful to me through the years and You have promised to never leave me nor forsake me. Not only have You saved me, but You have comforted and encouraged me when I needed it and have kept me on the straight and narrow path. It is my desire to stay close to You, Father. In view of all You have done and continue to do in my life, the least I should do is to present myself to You as a living and holy sacrifice. Oh, how I fail at this and ask for Your forgiveness. By Your grace, help me to die to myself, take up my cross daily, and follow You.

I am eternally grateful that I belong to You and will one day meet You face-to-face. Until that day, help me be Your faithful servant and give me a heart filled with thanksgiving for Who You are and all that You do. Thank You, Father, thank You, Jesus, and thank You, Holy Spirit. I desperately need You, my family needs You, and the world needs You. You are Lord of the nations and Your loving-kindness is spread abroad to everyone. Every person alive should praise You for Your merciful kindness and truth, which lasts forever. I praise You, Lord!

El Rachum ... The God of Compassion

The Lord is for me; I will not fear; what can man do to me?
Psalm 118:6

Prayer Response to Psalm 118

Good and merciful Lord, those who know You, love You and reverence You; they know Your mercies are new every day and Your character never changes. In times of distress I have prayed, and You have strengthened and encouraged me. When I am afraid, You remind me that I am not alone. You are right there with me and there is no need to be fearful.

In situations where others seem to be against me, I know I can trust You to work things out for Your honor and glory, and for my good. My confidence is in You because You are sovereign, know all things, and are in control of all things. You assure me that You love me.

The psalmist looked to You to deliver him from his enemies. His confidence was in Your power and strength, not his. All Your children are faced with spiritual enemies every day, and we need Your help, strength, and deliverance. Thank You for Jesus and the victory He has provided over sin and death. Thank You for the salvation that He alone provides. And thank You for Your Holy Spirit, Who indwells us and reminds us of Jesus and His commands, and Who also empowers us to obey Your Word.

I rejoice in Your salvation and the promise that I am secure in Jesus. I can even rejoice in times of discipline because Your Word tells me You discipline those whom You love. Your chastisement is never meant for harm but is always redemptive. Nothing happens in my life but what You allow, and You work it all out for my good. You are molding me and conforming me to be more like Jesus.

Thank You for opening my eyes so that I did not trip over Your cornerstone. Jesus was the cornerstone that most people rejected. Jesus is the Light of the World, and He was the perfect sinless sacrifice, which He Himself laid on the altar for my sin and the sins of the world. He is my Savior, and I praise You for such a glorious gift. Each day I praise You for Jesus and for saving my soul. You are a gracious and merciful Father.

El Malei Rachamim ... All Merciful God

How blessed are those whose way is blameless, who walk in the law of the Lord. How blessed are those who observe His testimonies, who seek Him with all their heart. Psalm 119:1–2

Prayer Response to Psalm 119 (1–40)

*A*uthor of the written Word, the psalmist has laid out how powerful and precious Your Word is and how it affects the lives of everyone who lives by it.

I praise and thank You that Your Word blesses my heart more and more as I strive to walk in Your ways and seek You. Obedience to Your Word will keep me from a shameful lifestyle, encourage thankfulness, and keep my heart right with You. Knowing Your Word and treasuring it in my heart will help protect me from sinful words, thoughts, and actions.

Continue to teach me so that I may be able to teach others. Your Word is a joy to me and gives me many things to meditate about. Reading and studying Your Word is a delight, and I pray that Your Holy Spirit will enable me to recall the Scriptures that I have stored in my heart. I do not want to forget them.

Each time I read the Bible, You reveal something new and different, and I am grateful that Your Word counsels, revives, and strengthens me. Give me understanding, the ability to discern truth, and enlarge my heart. It is my desire to continue to walk in obedience to Your Word, so please teach me.

Give me understanding and keep me from dishonest gain and vanity. Enable me to stand firm in Your Word so I will properly revere You, and please revive me by the power of Your righteous Word.

୧୨

Prayer Response to Psalm 119 (41–80)

*L*oving and kind Father, I praise and thank You for the salvation You have provided through Your Word. Jesus is the living Word and the gift of salvation to anyone who places their faith and trust in Him. Your written Word is all truth and I can trust all of it. I pray that You will keep that hunger and thirst for Your Word in my heart, and enable me to not only delight in it, but be able to apply it to my life.

Your Word instills hope and comforts me in times of distress. It lifts me up when I am in despair. Joy and singing are a byproduct of staying in Your Word, and I am learning to claim Your many promises as mine.

Father, You have been extremely gracious to me and have kept all Your promises. Help me to remain faithful and to focus on Your great love. Continue to teach me discernment and knowledge. I thank You for the things You have taught me, even when I strayed from Your Word. You created me, know everything about me, and know exactly what it takes to keep me right with You. Your judgments are perfect and right, and always redemptive. You are holy and righteous, yet also loving and compassionate. Keep me on Your straight and narrow path.

Prayer Response to Psalm 119 (81–120)

God of my salvation, Your Word provides great comfort and encouragement as I am bombarded daily with news from people who do not revere You or consider Your Word. Yet I know that You still sit on the throne and, one day, perfect judgment will be executed.

During these tumultuous days, I pray that I will continue to trust Your commands and seek You. Because I belong to You, I am confident that You will not leave nor forsake me.

I pray for those around the world who are being persecuted because they love You and Your Word. Strengthen them, encourage their hearts, grant them grace, and remind them of Your many promises and the hope they have in Jesus. Your Word is true and eternal and Your faithfulness continues throughout every generation.

Because I am weak and You are strong, I desperately need You. Your Word renews my mind and spirit and strengthens my heart. Reading it is a joy and a delight. Your Word gives me insight, wisdom, understanding, and keeps me from evil. The Bible is like a lamp which dispels the darkness and shows me the way. Oh Father, I pray that I will not forget Your Word or stray from it, no matter what happens. Keep me steadfast and sure until You take me home.

You, oh Lord, protect me. You are my hiding place and my shield. It is You Who sustains me through the power of Your Word. May I continue to have a healthy fear of You, and may I never be ashamed of the hope I have in Jesus.

❧

Prayer Response to Psalm 119 (121–152)

Sovereign Lord, You care about the needy and oppressed, and You alone can humble the proud who take advantage of others. Help me, Father, to leave righteous judgment in Your hands. You are merciful and righteous.

I need to keep learning from Your Word and I pray for greater understanding. You are a patient God, and I must learn that You act in accordance with Your will and timetable. The Bible is more precious than gold and every word in it is right and true. As I abide in Your Word, I gain understanding because You enlighten my heart and mind. Study of the Bible guides and protects me and keeps me from sin.

My heart aches for those who have no direction, because they do not love You or obey Your Word. Open their hearts and minds to see that You are a righteous, holy God, faithful and true. Your Word is truth without blemish, and I can put my faith and trust in it. Through Your Word I have learned about You, Jesus, salvation, Your kingdom, love, grace, faith, hope, mercy, reconciliation—the list is endless.

In the eyes of the world, my life is relatively insignificant, but the glorious truth is that I am a child of the King. In Christ, I stand before You as righteous and I belong to You. In times of trouble and distress, Your Word encourages my heart and gives me hope. In those nights when I cannot sleep, remind me of Your promises and give me a conscious awareness of Your presence. Let me hear Your voice; revive my spirit. Your Word assures me that when I draw near to You, You draw near to me. I trust Your Word because it is eternal. You are the same yesterday, today, and forever. Praise the Lord!

Prayer Response to Psalm 119 (153–176)

Omniscient God, You see and know all things and are aware of the afflictions that come to us all. Jesus said that in this life there will be many troubles. It is during those times that Your Word is most precious, as I cling to Your promises. They revive my heart and renew my mind.

There are many of Your children, around the world, experiencing terrible persecution, and I ask that You will remind them of Your truth which lasts forever. Strengthen them and help them claim every promise. May they not lose awe of Your Word or You.

I pray this for myself and my family and friends, when persecution does come. Wickedness and lies seem to be the norm, but, thankfully, I know I can trust Your Word. It alone is all truth. Within the pages of the Bible are great treasures, and I continue to praise You for the truths found there. Your Word gives me peace and keeps me steadfast. Over and over, You assure us that those who follow Your commands will not stumble.

Your Word reveals that salvation is found in Christ alone and that salvation is a gift to any and all who will believe and receive Jesus. My soul is secure in Him. I love Your Word because no matter what my circumstance is and no matter what my need is, Your Word provides me with the answer. Help me to always remember and love Your Word.

Immanuel ... God Is With Us

I will lift up my eyes to the mountains; from where shall my help come? My help comes from the Lord, who made heaven and earth. Psalm 121:1

Prayer Response to Psalm 120

Father, all of Your children, at some point, have been distressed over being falsely accused or misrepresented. We have also stressed over those who continue to lie to us and deceive us. It is in those times that we need to seek Your help. I ask for myself that You give me a spirit of forgiveness instead of anger and hurt, knowing that You alone can heal and change people. Only You know what is going on in their hearts and minds. When I encounter these situations, help me respond like Jesus, instead of react.

Lord, I know that lies and deceit are sins and that You hate all sin. But I also know that every sin can be forgiven, if confessed and repented. Remind me always to pray for those who continue in their deceitfulness. These encounters serve to remind me that this is a sinful world, and until Jesus returns it will not get better. Thankfully, I know this is not my home. Your children long for peace, the peace that only Jesus provides. I pray that those who create dissension will find peace in Christ.

El Emet ... The God of Truth

Prayer Response to Psalm 121

Creator and sustainer, it is You Who I look to daily, to lead and direct my life. Because You created all things including me, no one knows better than You, what I need. Why would I seek help from any other source?

Not only did You create me, but it is You Who continuously sustains me. You are always awake, alert, and attentive to my cries for help.

Just as You have protected, directed, and provided for Israel all these generations, You do the same for me and all Your children.

You are our firm foundation, and by Your power, keep us from stumbling. Day and night, You watch over us, guiding and protecting Your own. You are acutely aware of my coming and going, and You not only guide, but guard my way. You are always with me and my soul is secure in You. I praise and thank You!

El Chaiyai ... The God of My Life

Pray for the peace of Jerusalem: may they prosper who love you. Psalm 122:6

Prayer Response to Psalm 122

Omnipresent Lord, because Your Holy Spirit indwells me, I am aware I am always in Your presence. There is no place that I can go where You are not. However, like David, fellowshipping with You in Your house gives me great joy and delight. It is a place where I can hear Your Word preached, praise You with song, pray, give, fellowship with others, give thanks, and focus on You.

Jerusalem and, specifically the temple, were extremely important for the Israelites, who loved and obeyed You, because You met with them there. I pray that Your children would have that same longing and desire to meet in Your house today.

I pray for Israel, that their eyes would be enlightened to the truth, that Jesus is the Messiah and the cornerstone that they rejected. I continue to pray for their prosperity and peace, even though I know that true peace is only found in Christ. Reveal Your truth to their hearts and point them to Christ.

When Jesus returns, there will be peace on earth at last. I pray You will continue to protect Your purposes for Israel, as well as for Your children around the world. Help me to always pray for and seek Your best for others.

Immanuel ... God Is With Us

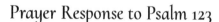

Prayer Response to Psalm 123

Sovereign Lord, You are high, uplifted, and enthroned in heaven. I look to You to meet my needs and I am so grateful for Your undeserved favor. You are my gracious Heavenly Father.

I pray for those who scoff at You and Your Word, for those who have become complacent and indifferent, and for those who are too proud to acknowledge that they need You.

I pray for my family and friends who continue to reject Your free gift of eternal life through Christ. Continue to pursue them and convict them of their sin, righteousness, and the judgment that is to come. Save them before it is too late!

El Hashamayim ... The God of the Heavens

Those who trust in the Lord are as Mount Zion, which cannot be moved but abides forever. Psalm 125:1

Prayer Response to Psalm 124

Lord, our protector, David understood that if it were not for Your divine strength, protection, and deliverance, Israel would not have survived as a nation. You called and established Israel, and continued to sustain them. David gave praise and honor to You and acknowledged You as Creator and Lord of heaven and earth.

Father, I, too, acknowledge Your sovereignty and lordship, and all Your attributes. I am humbled that You care about me and nothing escapes Your notice. I fully understand that I am created in Your image and dependent upon You for everything, including the air I breathe.

I thank You for guiding and directing my life, and for Your divine protection and intervention at times when I am unaware. When life is difficult, I know You are with me. You are the One I call upon for help in times of need.

El Roi ... The God Who Sees Me

Prayer Response to Psalm 125

You, oh Lord, are my sure foundation. My faith in Christ keeps me secure. You keep me from being restless, unstable, and inconsistent. Instead, You keep me strong, stable, and secure. As the mountains surround Jerusalem, so Your presence not only surrounds but indwells Your children. Thank You for Your protection from the ongoing evil all around us. Nothing can enter my life without Your permission.

David prayed that You would be good to the righteous, but I am thankful that Your goodness extends to everyone. You loved this unrighteous world enough to send Your Son Jesus to die for us so that through faith in Christ, we can be forgiven and have everlasting life. Jesus died for us while we were still sinners, and those who trust Him can stand before You, Father, just as if we had never sinned. Thank You, Jesus, for Your righteousness.

Israel rejected Jesus as Messiah, but I continue to pray that You will open their eyes to the truth. I pray for peace in Israel, but I know, in my heart of hearts, lasting peace will only happen when Jesus returns. Even so, come, Lord Jesus.

El Yisrael ... The God of Israel

Those who sow in tears shall reap with joyful shouting.
Psalm 126:5

Prayer Response to Psalm 126

Gracious and merciful Father, like the psalmist, I praise You with laughter and singing for all You have done and are doing in my life. Your goodness exceeds my expectations.

The children of Israel had heard prophecies regarding restoration, and the reality of those promises brought joy unspeakable! There are many ways that You give me joy; the greatest joy is the salvation You provided for me through my faith in Jesus. In Christ, I have the joy of fellowship with You and other believers. Serving You with my talents and gifts is a joy and delight. And then there is the joy of spiritual victories. Despite times of sadness and weeping, joy always follows.

As I continue to pray for and weep over those I love who are still doubtful or have rejected Jesus as Lord and Savior, I know You have heard my prayers and are working in their lives. Sowing the seeds of the Gospel is tedious and requires special care. They need to be continually watered and cared for, and then I patiently wait. Help me, Father, not to grow weary in doing good. You promise a harvest if I do not give up.

Jesus was a man of sorrows, sowing the seeds of the Gospel. When He comes again, He will be bringing His sheaves with Him. Thank You for allowing me to be one of them.

El Yeshuatenu ... The God of Our Salvation

Prayer Response to Psalm 127

Heavenly Father, You are my Savior and Lord. I acknowledge that anything I do must have Your blessing; otherwise, all of it will be done in vain. The builder and the watchman are equally dependent upon You to do the job well.

Solomon recognized the vanity of life apart from You. Forgive me when I depend upon my own strength to accomplish what only You can do. Life is more than just rising early, working hard all day, and dealing with the sorrows of life. You give life meaning, purpose, and fulfillment when we acknowledge You and seek Your will and direction. Each night, when I lay my head on the pillow, I am grateful for the time of rest and recognize it as a gift from You.

I praise and thank You for my children and grandchildren. They are a joy and delight, even though there are many heartaches that come with them. They are Your gift to me. My family is small, but the older I get, the more I appreciate their love and support. Family is extremely important to me and I love each of them dearly. Some are closer and more responsive, but I continue to lift each one to You daily, asking You to draw them into a closer relationship with You. That must start with recognizing their sinful nature and need for a Savior, confessing their sin and repenting, believing and receiving Jesus as Savior and Lord, and allowing Him to cleanse, purify, and restore.

When all is said and done, when we take our last breath, the only thing that will really matter is whether or not we know Jesus. I pray for Your mercy and grace.

El Chaiyai ... The God of My Life

How blessed is everyone who fears the Lord, who walks in His ways. Psalm 128:1

Prayer Response to Psalm 128

Jehovah Jireh, You are Creator of heaven and earth and sustainer of all things. It is You Who provides for all of creation. I praise You for Your awesomeness and thank You for the many blessings You freely give.

You have created man in Your image, and have provided Your Word to guide and instruct us in how we are to live. You are the author and finisher of my faith, and obedience to Your Word is the key to an abundant life. Please keep me on the straight and narrow path and help me to always walk in Your ways. Keep my heart in tune with Yours.

As I read the blessings described regarding family, I realize that this is the ideal goal: Enjoying the fruit of our labor, and a home where husband, wife, and children are in a right relationship with You. Because we all have free will, not every home is blessed in this way. One person out of fellowship with You in a family, or within the church body, upsets the peace and unity, and we must seek Your forgiveness, cleansing, and restoration.

I pray for my family and ask that You continue to reveal to them their need for Jesus, and to heal the deep wounds of their hearts. Jesus came to seek and save the lost, but He also said that in Him we have abundant life and eternal life. Your Word repeatedly tells us that a healthy, reverent fear of You is the beginning of wisdom. I thank You for my children and grandchildren and the gift they are to me. You know where they are in their relationship with You. It is not Your will that any should perish, but their wills must submit to Yours.

The psalmist prayed for Israel and, especially, for peace. I, too, pray for the peace of Israel, and the United States of America. I do know that true peace can only be found in Jesus, the Prince of Peace. Even so, come, Lord Jesus.

El Channun ... The Gracious God

O Israel, hope in the Lord; for with the Lord there is loving-kindness, and with Him is abundant redemption. Psalm 130:7

Prayer Response to Psalm 129

God of Israel, from the nation's inception, Israel has endured unique and evil inflictions. Nations have continued to despise Your chosen people, but no one has succeeded in wiping them out. Though they have suffered immensely as a nation, You have remained faithful to Your covenant with them and have preserved them as a nation. I praise and thank You for Your faithfulness.

The psalmist prays for You to judge those who plot against Israel. You, oh Lord, are sovereign over all nations, and You have a purpose and plan, and Your ways are not ours. I know from Your Word that You are righteous and just and nothing escapes Your attention.

One day, Jesus will return, and true righteousness and justice will reign in Israel. But until then, I pray that You will protect Your chosen people and that You will open their hearts and minds to see that Jesus was, and is, the promised Messiah that they did not recognize. They will know this truth when Jesus comes again, but until then, protect Your plans and purposes for them as a nation.

El Yisrael ... The God of Israel

Prayer Response to Psalm 130

God of all comfort, on more than one occasion I have been in deep distress, with no place to turn but to You. You are always with me—seeing, knowing, watching, and hearing. How blessed I am that I can always rely on Your unchanging faithfulness. I am humbled that You, a holy God, loved me enough to send Your Son Jesus to die for my sin. Such love is far beyond my comprehension.

Grant me a better understanding and pour out Your love into, and out of, my heart. I praise and thank You for the forgiveness of sin that Jesus provides, and help me to forgive others as You have forgiven me.

I praise You for Your love, grace, and mercy, and I pray that my life will point others to Jesus so they, too, can experience Your forgiveness and joy, and experience eternal life. I would be lost without You. My hope is in Jesus. In Him there is mercy, grace, and redemption for all who will place their faith and trust in Him. How can anyone reject such a gracious gift!

May Israel place their hope in You.

El Erekh Apayim avi ha-Tanchumim ...
The God of Patience and Consolation

O Israel, hope in the Lord from this time forth and forever.
Psalm 131:3

Prayer Response to Psalm 131

Most gracious Heavenly Father, Your Word has much to say about the dangers of pride and Your contempt toward it. Pride is an area that Your children struggle with. Forgive me for the pride in my own heart that continues to show its ugly head. Oh Father, help me to reject all pride and to walk in humility before You and others. Pride shows up in spiritual matters when I become too focused on my own spirituality. It also becomes evident when I focus on my intellectual abilities. Remind me often to focus on You first, others second, and myself last.

It is my desire to stay close to You so that my heart is at peace and content with who I am in Christ. I do not have to be self-sufficient or the best at anything, but I do need to submit to Your will for my life and *be* the person You have created me to be.

You know that one of my weaknesses is worrying about what others think. I pray for power to overcome because deep down I know that the only person I need to please is You. My hope is in Jesus. I cannot trust myself, my wisdom or power, nor anyone else's.

You alone are faithful, from everlasting to everlasting. You are my Heavenly Father and I am Your child. Help me to act like Your child in every area of life.

El Yeshuati ... The God of My Salvation

For the Lord has chosen Zion; He has desired it for His habitation. Psalm 132:13

Prayer Response to Psalm 132

God of my past, present, and future, the psalmist is asking God to remember the past afflictions of His servant David. Your Word reveals that nothing escapes You and that You are acutely aware of all things in each person's life. Your Word indicates that there are books in which details of our lives are recorded. You do not forget. David was a man after Your heart, although he suffered many things.

My life and the lives of all Your children are wrought with pain and sorrow. Jesus told us that would be the case because we live in a sin-cursed world. But Jesus told us to take cheer because He came and has overcome the world. Thank You for the victory and the hope I have in Jesus.

It is my desire to be like David; I want to be a woman after Your heart. David loved You so much and his heart's desire was to rebuild the temple. You blessed him with so many good things, including a palace, he thought it only right that Your dwelling should be the finest. However, it was not Your will for him to build Your temple.

Sometimes, in my exuberance there are so many things that I desire to do, yet I know there are specific works You have created for me to do. I must learn to be content with Your will for my life.

David was not able to build the temple, but it was through David's bloodline that Jesus came. This was an even greater blessing! Jerusalem was Your chosen place to dwell among Your chosen people, and You promised Your blessing. Ultimately, Messiah would come out of the Jewish nation and Jesus was born.

David was a godly king, but his kingdom ended. Jesus came, and His kingdom will never end because His kingdom is everlasting. The Jewish nation at large rejected Jesus as Messiah, and the world at large continues to reject Him as Savior.

But what joy and hope You have given me and everyone else who has received Your free gift of salvation through faith in Christ! Your

Word is clear: Jesus is coming again. This time He will come to judge the earth and set up His kingdom, and He will reign with perfect justice, righteousness, and peace. Until that day, I pray that I will remain faithful.

El De'ot ... The God of Knowledge

Behold, how good and how pleasant it is for brothers to dwell together in unity! Psalm 133:1

Prayer Response to Psalms 133–134

Triune God, David recognized the importance of unity among Your children and described just how precious it is. The necessity of the unity of the Spirit continues into the New Testament. Jesus prayed that we would be one, just as He was one with You.

Father, we can only have unity to the degree that our relationship with You is where it should be. Please forgive me, forgive Your children, when we allow sin to disrupt that unity. You, the Father, Jesus the Son, and the Holy Spirit are one and work in perfect harmony. Because Your Holy Spirit indwells each believer, we, too, should operate in perfect unity. Only You, Lord, can maintain that unity, and that is my prayer for Your church.

May all Your children serve You with the gifts and abilities that You have given, and we all bless and praise You for Who You are and the many ways You bless us. Isaiah 43:7 says: "Everyone who is called by My name, whom I created for My glory, whom I formed and made …" Help each of us remember that our sole purpose is to bring honor and glory to You, and Your Word provides the details of how we accomplish that.

Thank You for Your patience with me and for the forgiveness I have in Christ, because I daily fall short of Your glory. Strengthen me, continue to teach and mold me, cleanse me, and fill me with Your Spirit so I can be more like Jesus. Pour out Your love into my heart so others will know I belong to You and will desire to know that same love. Apart from Jesus, I can do nothing.

El Hakkavod ... The God of Glory

For I know that the Lord is great and that our Lord is above all gods. Psalm 135:5

Prayer Response to Psalm 135

Creator and Redeemer, as Your child I am compelled to praise You simply for Who You are. You have created and redeemed me, and Your character and attributes are deserving of my praise. Because of Your goodness, I am chosen to be Your child and it gives me great pleasure to give You praise and thanks.

Your greatness is seen in the heavens, on the earth, and in the seas. You are the sovereign God and there is no other. It is You Who controls the wind, the lightning, and the rain, and it is You Who is Lord of the nations.

As in the days of old, You watch over, guide, direct, and protect Your children. You defeated the enemies of Israel and redeemed the Israelites from bondage over and over again. Thank You for redeeming me from my spiritual enemy and a life of sin.

Thank You for Jesus, Who made my salvation possible. You are a holy God and hate sin. In fact, Your Word tells us that the wages of sin is death. But You are also loving and merciful and have provided redemption for anyone who will believe and receive Jesus Christ as their Lord and Savior.

So many things in this world bring pleasure, and sometimes, Lord, Your children idolize things without giving thought to the fact that without You, none of it would exist. Forgive me for the idols of my heart, and help others to see that our trust must be in You because You are everlasting and the things of this world are all passing away.

I often meditate on this fact: When I take my last breath, the only thing that will matter is my personal relationship with You, through Jesus. Thank You for imparting to me a holy fear of Your awesome power and greatness.

I praise You for revealing to me my sin and my need for a Savior and the grace gift of faith, to believe and receive Your gift of salvation. Thank You, Jesus, for laying down Your life for mine and for the gift of eternal life. I bless and praise Your holy name.

El Hannora ... The Awesome God

Give thanks to the Lord of lords, for His lovingkindness is everlasting. Psalm 136:3

Prayer Response to Psalm 136

Loving and kind Father, this Psalm reminds me to meditate on Your goodness, kindness, and love—all undeserved by me. You are my Lord and Savior, and Your love and kindness are everlasting.

It goes without saying that Your greatness and power are revealed daily as I observe all that You have created. The land and sea, sun, moon, and stars, all the living plants and animals, and mankind are evidence that You are God Almighty. You created it all, sustain it all, and it all functions as You ordained.

The psalmist praised You for the ways You miraculously guided, directed, and protected Israel. I, too, praise You for Your providential care. You have always provided for my needs and so much more. Forgive me for the times I take Your goodness for granted.

I periodically look back on my life and can see Your guiding hand in all of it, even the painful circumstances of life. Your promise to me is that You cause all things to work together for my good. Your love for me is far beyond my comprehension, yet I thank You and praise You for it.

Your love is so grand that it extends to everyone. You sent Your Son Jesus to die on a cross, to pay the penalty for sin. And everyone who believes and receives Your gift of salvation through Jesus is forgiven and has eternal life. How can anyone reject such a wonderful gift! Thank You, Jesus, for dying for me and saving my soul. You are good, loving, and kind, and from everlasting to everlasting.

El Olam ... The Everlasting God

By the rivers of Babylon, there we sat down and wept, when we remembered Zion. Psalm 137:1

Prayer Response to Psalm 137

Holy and righteous God, this Psalm reminds me that You are holy and all sin is abhorrent to You. Because of Who You are, sin must be judged.

The psalmist is mourning Israel's captivity in Babylon, which was Your judgment against their sinfulness and rebellion. As the Israelites gathered by the rivers to worship, they remembered the good old days in the Promised Land and longed for the songs of Zion.

For myself, I pray that I will not stray from Your truth, that You will guard my heart and mind, and enable me to stay on course. For my country, I confess our rebellion against You and ask for Your forgiveness. I seek Your mercy and grace and an outpouring of Your spirit. I pray that Your people will humble themselves, repent, and seek You, and that You will heal our land. I pray that we will be spared the heartaches of unnecessary death, loss of property, destruction, captivity, cruelty, and the loss of joy.

Sin brings heartache and separation from You, and the only way to be restored is confession and repentance. Dear God, help me to keep short accounts with You. When I do falter and fail, Holy Spirit, remind me that Jesus died so that my sins are forgiven, and if I confess them, He is faithful and will forgive my sin and restore my fellowship with You. I am thankful that Your Holy Spirit resides within me, so that no matter where I am in this world, I can maintain fellowship with You through Jesus.

Lord, even if our country were to be taken into captivity, You promise to never leave nor forsake Your children. You also promise that You cause all things to work together for our good. You are sovereign and You always judge rightly. You sometimes use our enemies to discipline us, but they, too, are accountable to You. Just as parents love their children and discipline them, You love Your children and discipline us. It is always done in love and with the purpose of reconciliation and restoration.

Thank You for being my loving Heavenly Father. I pray for my loved ones and others who do not have a personal relationship with You. Replace their heart of stone with a heart of flesh and draw them to Jesus.

El Tsaddik ... The Righteous God

Though I walk in the midst of trouble, You will revive me; ...
Psalm 138:7

Prayer Response to Psalm 138

Giver of life and every good and perfect gift, You are God of creation and Lord of my life. I praise and thank You for the undeserved blessings You bestow. You alone are worthy of my worship and praise.

First, I thank You for Your love, which is greater than my understanding. You sent Jesus to die on the cross so that my sins and the sins of a lost and dying world can have forgiveness and obtain everlasting life. There is no greater love than this.

I experience Your kindness daily, in the most ordinary and extraordinary ways. Your Word is my treasure house; it ministers to my soul each time I read it. The Bible strengthens, encourages, exhorts, revives, comforts, teaches, enlightens, counsels, sustains, establishes, restrains, delivers, purifies, imparts knowledge and discernment, gives joy and grace, makes me thankful, enlarges my heart, keeps me honest, makes me wise, gives insight and direction, keeps me from sin, and keeps me close to You.

When I pray, You listen and answer my prayers according to Your will and timing. You strengthen my inner person and grant me the boldness to do and say the things You ask me to. Forgive me for the times I fail to submit. I pray for our world leaders because they need to acknowledge and submit to You, instead of reveling in their own arrogance and pride! One day they will! In fact, one day every person will acknowledge You as Lord and give You the glory You deserve. Come, Lord Jesus!

I can praise You that even during the midst of tough times, I belong to You and nothing happens unless You allow it. Remind me that You always have a divine purpose. You began the work of salvation in my life and it is You Who will complete it. I am perfectly secure in Jesus. Nothing and no one can snatch me out of His hand, and You have promised to never leave me nor forsake me. Your mercies are new every morning, and Your loving-kindness is everlasting. Hallelujah!

El Hanne'eman ... The Faithful God

Search me, O God, and know my heart; try me and know my
anxious thoughts; and see if there be any hurtful way in me,
and lead me in the everlasting way. Psalm 139:23–24

Prayer Response to Psalm 139

Omniscient, omnipresent, and omnipotent God, this Psalm encourages my heart and gives me great comfort; it reminds me that You know every detail of my life. You understand and know me better than I know myself. You know my thoughts and every word I am going to speak before I open my mouth, and You are aware of every step I take. My mind cannot comprehend such wisdom and knowledge. It is also incomprehensible that You see and know all things. I cannot grasp that Your presence cannot be escaped because You are everywhere!

Though I do not understand it, I am grateful for Your ever-abiding presence. Your Spirit is ever with me, guiding and directing my steps. Even in the dark times of life, You are my Light Who lights the way. You never leave me, no matter where I go. Your awesome power is too grand for me to fully grasp.

I am awed that You knew me before I was born. You created and uniquely fashioned me in my mother's womb and before my birth You ordained how long I will live on this earth. I am a walking miracle! How awesome You are!

Because my heart is deceitful and I may not even know it, I must depend upon You to reveal the sin that lies deep within. Like David, I ask that You search my heart and reveal to me those things of which I need to confess and repent. Sin causes a separation from You, and I long to maintain fellowship with You, and others. Keep me on Your righteous path and close to You. Thank You for life everlasting.

El Roi ... The God Who Sees Me

I know that the Lord will maintain the cause of the afflicted and justice for the poor. Psalm 140:12

Prayer Response to Psalm 140

Redeemer and sustainer, Your Word is clear that all mankind has a sin problem, and that is why there is violence, wars, and hateful speech. I pray for Your divine protection in this sin-cursed world, for all Your children. I praise You for Jesus, Who sacrificed His life for mine so that I am forgiven and changed. Only Jesus can change the wicked heart, save a soul, and impute righteousness. Christ did everything necessary to save the sins of a lost and wicked world. Those who believe and receive Him are new creations and have been given eternal life.

I pray for the vast majority of people who continue to reject Jesus. Thank You for Your great salvation and the victory I enjoy in Christ. Because I belong to You, I know You are always with me and nothing can happen in my life unless You allow it. You guide, direct, and protect me, and there is no need to fear what others may say, think, or do. All peoples are accountable to You, whether they acknowledge it or not.

You are compassionate and merciful, and provide justice for the poor and afflicted. You are also holy and righteous, and will not let wickedness go unpunished indefinitely.

I praise and thank You for Your indwelling Holy Spirit, Your ever-abiding presence. Hallelujah!

El Chaiyai ... The God of My Life

Set a guard, O Lord, over my mouth; keep watch over the door of my lips. Do not incline my heart to any evil thing ...
Psalm 141:3–4

Prayer Response to Psalm 141

My Lord and Savior, how precious it is to think that my prayers are pleasing to You. They are like the aroma of burning incense. Fill my heart and my mind with the thoughts and words to speak. I know that my heart is deceitful, so I ask that You will guard my heart and my mind, and that my words will be pleasing to You. I acknowledge that I am a sinner by nature, but my desire is to live my life in a way that honors You.

Place others in my life who love You and are willing to help keep me accountable for my actions, words, and attitudes. Help me accept their counsel and exhortations as coming from You.

I always thank You for Your Word because it instructs me in Your ways, and encourages, comforts, and admonishes me. Enable me to be a submissive and obedient servant.

Father, evil is everywhere, and I confess that it sometimes overwhelms me. Only You can convince people of their sin and their need for salvation. You are holy and righteous and Your judgments are pure. Just as I trust You to take care of me, I trust that You will deal with the unrighteous in Your perfect timing and way. It is not Your desire that any should perish, but the choice belongs to each individual. Those who continue in their sin many times fall into their own sinful trap. You have warned us that we do indeed reap the things we sow.

Thank You, Jesus, for the difference You make in my life. I continue to pray for my loved ones who do not have a relationship with You. Do the necessary work in their hearts, enable them to see Your great love and forgiveness, and give them a desire to accept Your glorious gift of salvation. Thank You for saving me. I am secure in You.

El Yeshuati ... The God of My Salvation

For the sake of Your name, O Lord, revive me ... Psalm 143:11

Prayer Response to Psalms 142–143

God of compassion and mercy, I know I am not supposed to complain, but when I am overwhelmed with life and bring my complaints to You, You hear and listen. When no one else seems to care, I know You do. You are my refuge and strength, and only You can give me victory through life's struggles.

I thank You for godly people that You have placed in my life, who encourage me and pray for me. They are gifts of grace from You. In times of struggle, You may deliver me or You will give me Your strength and power to overcome. I trust You because You have always been gracious to me. I remember the ways You have been there for me in the past, and I meditate on Your goodness and power.

By Your Word, You teach me the way I should take, and my heart and soul long for You. You are loving and kind, and Your mercies are new each day. You are faithful and righteous in all Your ways and, although I am not righteous, Jesus has imputed to me His righteousness. Therefore I can come boldly into Your presence.

Continue to teach me Your will and enable me to be obedient. I pray that Your Spirit will continue to lead and guide me and keep me steadfast.

O God, in times of distress, I ask that You revive my soul, for Your name's sake. Help me, Father, to wait upon You because I belong to You.

El Rachum ... The God of Compassion

How blessed are the people whose God is the Lord!
Psalm 144:15

Prayer Response to Psalm 144

Lord, You are my all in all. You are my Rock and fortress, and have provided the weapons I need to combat the spiritual warfare I face daily. You have saved me through faith in Christ, and He has imputed to me His righteousness. He is my high tower and deliverer. He is my shield and refuge. It is You Who has given me faith to believe and trust You. And it is Your Word that instructs me in all my ways. Your truth guides and directs me as I carry the gospel of peace out into the world.

I am an unworthy vessel and my days on earth are short. Yet You love me and care for my needs. In this life, there will continue to be struggles. Jesus warned us that this would be true, so my victory is found in Him.

You are all-powerful, all-knowing, all-seeing, and completely sovereign. I trust You to sustain me and to deal with others in accordance with Your perfect plan and will.

I praise and thank You for the times that You have lifted me out of despair and put a new song in my heart. You, O Lord, are my salvation and joy. I praise You for the times You have delivered me from difficult situations and for the times that You did not. In those times, You provided strength, mercy, and grace, and reminded me that You cause all things to work out for my good.

You also reminded me that the afflictions of this world are temporary and heaven will be free of all heartache, pain, and death. I look forward to the day when sin is no more and I see Jesus face-to-face. Until then, I continue to pray that You will abundantly bless those who love You, and provide for their needs. For those who do not have a personal relationship with You through Christ, I pray for their salvation. True joy and peace are only found in Jesus. Thank You, Jesus, for saving my soul.

El Shaddai ... The All-Sufficient God

The Lord is gracious and merciful; slow to anger and great in lovingkindness. Psalm 145:8

Prayer Response to Psalm 145

Gracious and merciful Lord, I choose to praise You each day simply because of Who You are. You are God Almighty, King of Kings, and Lord of Lords. Your greatness exceeds my imagination, and You are worthy of my praise. It is my prayer that my children and grandchildren will learn to praise You, as well. Not only do I need to meditate upon Your majesty and glory and all the wonderful things You do, but I need to share these things with family and friends and others whom You place in my life. The things You teach me are things I must share with others. Everyone needs to know that You are gracious and compassionate, slow to anger, and merciful. Your mercies are evident in Your goodness to all.

All of creation declares Your glory, and those who trust You and love You praise and bless Your name. Grant me boldness in speaking to others about Your power and about Your kingdom. Enable me to be a messenger of Your grace and love.

Jesus came that we might have life and have it abundantly. He came that we might have everlasting life in Your kingdom. Help me to faithfully share the love of Jesus with a lost and dying world.

Father, I am thankful that You sustain me and encourage my heart when I am discouraged. Your watchful eye is ever looking over me and You faithfully provide for my needs. It is You Who satisfies the deep needs of my heart. You are righteous in all Your ways and far more gracious than I could ever deserve.

You are always with me and attentive to my prayers, answering each one in accordance with Your will. I belong to You and You will complete the work You began in my life. I am secure in You. May I forever praise You and continue to pray for those who continue to reject You. One day, every tongue will praise and bless Your name.

El-Channun ... The Gracious God

I will praise the Lord while I live; I will sing praises to my God while I have my being. Psalm 146:2

Prayer Response to Psalm 146

God Almighty and sovereign Lord, I do praise You for Who You are and all Your miraculous works. I pray that I will make a concious effort to praise You in every circumstance of life, as long as I have breath to do so. You alone are trustworthy and only You provide salvation for mankind.

Mere man is but a vapor and limited in what can be accomplished; eventually, he dies and is forgotten. All thoughts and plans die with him. But You, O Lord, are from everlasting to everlasting. My trust and hope are in You, Creator of heaven and earth. It is You Who opened my eyes to the truth of Your Word; You gave me the faith to believe in Jesus so that I possess eternal salvation.

Lord, You care for the oppressed and provide for the hungry. You heal the blind and encourage the downtrodden. You offer protection to strangers and support those who cannot defend themselves. You love the righteous and thwart the devices of evil.

How thankful I am that You set the captives free! Not everyone realizes that we are all in bondage by our sin, but You sent Your Son Jesus to set us free from that bondage. In Him there is forgiveness, salvation, abundant life, and life eternal. I am a new creation in Christ, and I thank You for Your gracious salvation. I praise You that Your kingdom is everlasting and that You will reign as Lord and King forever! Hallelujah!

El Gibbor ... The Mighty God

Great is our Lord and abundant in strength; His understanding is infinite. Psalm 147:5

Prayer Response to Psalm 147

lmighty God and Lord, it is only right and fitting that Your children give You the praise and honor You deserve. Praise is not only beautiful to You, but is also pleasant and beautiful to the ones who praise and to those who listen. Throughout these Psalms there have been many reasons listed to praise You. This one is no different.

You have preserved a chosen nation and made it strong. You minister to the outcasts and heal the brokenhearted and wounded. It is hard to imagine, but You even know the number of stars in the sky and call each of them by name! Your might and power are too great for me to comprehend, and Your wisdom and understanding are infinite. You reach out and lift the humble and execute justice to those who reject You. This is opposite from the world. The world has disdain for the meek and exalts the wicked. You resist the proud and give grace to the humble.

You created the heavens, cause it to rain, make the grass grow, and provide food for the animals and birds. I choose to praise and thank You for Your goodness—in word, in song, and with instruments. When You created the heavens and the earth and filled it with vegetation, animals, and man, You said it was good, and it is. However, Your delight is in those who reverence, trust, and obey You.

Israel had many reasons to praise You. You strengthened their borders, blessed their children, gave them peace, and provided for their needs.

Your majesty is also evident in that You control the atmosphere: the wind, rain, snow, hail, frost, heat, cold, and the waters. You control and sustain it all! Your goodness is shown to all mankind, but especially to Israel, Your chosen nation. You have kept Your covenant with Israel even though they rebelled against You over and over. They even rejected Jesus, the long-awaited Messiah. Open their hearts and minds and reveal to them the truth of Your Word. They were chosen to be a light to the nations, and though they have failed to be that light, they are still Your chosen people. In this life, I will never be able to fully comprehend Your love, mercy, grace, and forgiveness, but I can spend the rest of my days praising You for Who You are. Praise the Lord!

El Hannora ... The Awesome God

For the Lord takes pleasure in His people; He will beautify the afflicted ones with salvation. Psalm 149:4

Prayer Response to Psalms 148–150

Heavenly Father, Savior and Lord, these last three Psalms are pure praise to You. They express who and what should praise You, where to praise You, and how. Starting from heaven itself, the angels, sun, moon, and stars all resound praise to You. After all, by Your spoken word, they were created and are continually sustained by You.

You established the earth and spoke all things into being, and it all reveals Your majesty. The mountains, trees, animals, creeping things, things that fly, things that live in the sea, and even the wind, fire, hail, and snow all point to an awesome and miraculous God.

All people, regardless of age or status, should praise You because You are our Maker and sustainer. Without You, we would not exist; we are dependent upon You for the very air we breathe. Every created thing was created with precision and order, and for Your pleasure.

We can praise You with song and dancing, and with all the different musical instruments. Praise to You can be individual or communal, in Your sanctuary or anyplace in the universe, because You are everywhere.

We praise You because You take pleasure in Your people. You loved us enough to provide salvation to anyone who will believe and receive Your gracious gift. What a loving, merciful, and gracious God and Father!

You are praised because You are holy and righteous, and will one day right all the wrongs and will reign in perfect righteousness!

As I have prayed though these Psalms, Lord, I hope that I have magnified and honored You the way You deserve. Praising You keeps me humble and increases my faith. It motivates me to be more like Jesus and to live a life that pleases You. Praise encourages my heart and increases my joy. It is only fitting that I end with "Let everything that has breath, praise the Lord. Praise the Lord!" (Psalm 150:6) Amen!

El Shaddai ... The All-Sufficient God

Afterword

From beginning to end, the Bible reveals an awesome God Who takes great delight and care in His creation. God Almighty created it all and sustains it all. He created man in His image, and until the first man, Adam, sinned and disobeyed God, there was sweet fellowship between God and man. Sin separated mankind from fellowship with God because God is righteous and holy and cannot tolerate sin. But because of His great love, God Himself pursued mankind and provided a way for people to be reconciled to Him.

In the Old Testament, God accepted animal sacrifices which, if performed according to His instructions, would provide forgiveness and a right standing with God. God also provided the Ten Commandments as a standard to live by, which would enable people to maintain a right standing with Him and others—only if the commandments were obeyed. Unfortunately, no one was able to live up to these standards, and the heart and nature of man was not changed.

God also instituted priests, who would intercede to God on behalf of the people. He also sent prophets to exhort and warn when the people turned away from Him. But the prophets also foretold of a Messiah, a King Who would redeem His people. The Messiah did come, but the world at large rejected Him because Jesus did not come as a conquering king but as a suffering Savior.

In spite of all the prophesies that Jesus fulfilled, He was not well received, even by the religious elite. "But as many as received Him, to them He gave the right to become children of God, even to those who believe in His name." (John 1:12) Jesus came as the perfect and sinless Lamb of God, and made the ultimate sacrifice of Himself so that we might be forgiven and our relationship with God restored.

The Bible makes it clear that we are all sinners. Romans 3:23 states: "For all have sinned and fall short of the glory of God." It further says, in Romans 6:23: "For the wages of sin is death, but the free gift of God is eternal life in Christ Jesus our Lord." In John 10:9, Jesus says, "I am the door; if anyone enters through Me, he will be saved." And in verse 28 of that same chapter, Jesus says, "I give eternal life to them, and they will never perish; and no one will snatch them out of My hand."

We can never earn our salvation, no matter how many great things we do. Salvation is God's gift to us. However, we must receive it before we can possess it. How can anyone reject such love! "For God so loved the world, that He gave His only begotten Son, that whoever *believes* in Him shall not perish, but have eternal life." (John 3:16) Praise be to God for His gracious and glorious gift! Will you pray and receive Jesus today?

Jesus said, "I am the way, and the truth, and the life; no one comes to the Father but through Me." John 14:6

Words from the Author

I was inspired to write *Praying Through the Psalms* because I want to share with others what I learned years ago: Bible reading and prayer go hand in hand. In order to strengthen and maintain our relationship with the Lord, spending time with Him is crucial. He speaks to us through His written Word and we respond to Him through prayer.

The Psalms is a book of praise which reveals numerous reasons to praise and give thanks to God. Creation is one reason.

In this book, I have included over one hundred majestic sunrise photos that I have captured on camera. Each one reflects God's majesty. As you meditate, reflect, and pray through each Psalm, I am confident that you will be encouraged, your faith strengthened, your worship refreshed, your heart and mind quieted, and your spirit lifted.

CPSIA information can be obtained
at www.ICGtesting.com
Printed in the USA
LVHW011320060821
694665LV00005B/10